6R30

John Ohnesorge
Harvard Law School
1997

Jame T
Clare
1 November 1976.

OP

9⁰⁻

pencil
underlining

Discretionary Justice in Europe and America

Discretionary Justice
in Europe and America

Kenneth Culp Davis

and European Associates

LARS BUSCK

SABINO CASSESE

JOACHIM HERRMANN

KARL MATTHIAS MEESSEN

CHRISTIAN MERLIN

A. B. RINGELING

J. A. J. SCHEFFERS

A. A. M. F. STAATSEN

R. P. WOLTERS

University of Illinois Press
Urbana Chicago London

LIBRARY OF CONGRESS CATALOGING IN PUBLICATION DATA

Davis, Kenneth Culp.
    Discretionary justice in Europe and America.

    Includes bibliographical references.
    1. Administrative discretion—Europe.   2. Judicial
discretion—Europe.   3. Administrative discretion—United
States.   4. Judicial discretion—United States.   I. Title.
Law   340.1'1   75-38842
ISBN 0-252-00579-1

Contributors

LARS BUSCK, Assistant Professor of Law, University of Copenhagen

SABINO CASSESE, Professor of Law, University of Naples

KENNETH CULP DAVIS, John P. Wilson Professor of Law, University of Chicago

JOACHIM HERRMANN, Professor of Law, University of Augsburg

KARL MATTHIAS MEESSEN, Professor of Law, University of Bonn

CHRISTIAN MERLIN, Graduate of University of Paris Faculty of Law

A. A. M. F. STAATSEN, Formerly Assistant Professor, University of Groningen, now Ministry of Health and Environment

A. B. RINGELING, J. A. J. SCHEFFERS, and R. P. WOLTERS, all assistants of Professor S. F. L. Baron van Wijnbergen, Katholieke University, Nijmegen

Preface

This symposium is based on my book entitled *Discretionary Justice: A Preliminary Inquiry* (1969), in which I found many problems about governmental discretion that Americans had inadequately solved. Curious about the extent to which the rest of the world may have solved them, I searched for the results of empirical investigations in Europe. Finding none, I decided to take some samples of exercise of discretionary power in Europe. With a grant from the Ford Foundation, I employed the nine collaborators who have written the eight European essays in this volume. Each essay is entirely its author's; I have counseled and I have edited the English (in which the essayists have varying skills), but I have not sought to control the substance or the ideas.

My introductory chapter explains the subjects of the inquiry, its objectives, background, and method. After each European essay I have provided an American commentary, usually drawing American comparisons or contrasts, and freely expressing the opinion of one with an American background. By far the most important such commentary, addressed especially to Americans, is the one on the German prosecutor. My concluding chapter does not attempt to summarize the numerous ideas that appear throughout the symposium but is limited to two major conclusions, the first intended especially for Americans and the second for Europeans.

Acknowledgments. My greatest indebtedness, of course, is to my nine European collaborators, who have brought talent, skill, and patience to the challenging tasks of carrying out this foreigner's odd notions of what to do and how to do it. Our principal senior adviser from Europe has been Professor Bent Christensen of the University of Copenhagen, whose wise counsel at all stages of the project has been invaluable. We are also grateful to Professor S. F. L. Baron van Wijnbergen of Katholieke University, Nijmegen, the Netherlands, who served as an adviser at our 1971 Paris meeting and at our 1972 Amsterdam meeting, and to Professor Roland Drago of the University of Paris, who served as an adviser at our Paris meeting. My colleague at the University of Chicago, Professor Max Rheinstein, on innumerable occasions has helped me through perplexities of European strangeness, and in the concluding stages my colleague, Professor James Beardsley, who has practiced in Paris, has helped me to understand some aspects of French law. Also in the concluding stages, Judge Ernst Pakuscher, formerly of the West German Administrative Court and now of the Patent Court, has advised me about European administrative law.

My collaborators and I are all grateful to the Ford Foundation for financial support.

—K. C. D.

Contents

Discretionary Justice in Europe and America

CHAPTER ONE

The Inquiry—the Subject, Objectives, Background, and Method

KENNETH CULP DAVIS

The Subject

In all advanced nations of the world, justice is administered more outside courts than in them. This symposium of essays is concerned with improving the quality of justice that is administered outside courts by such officers as prosecutors, welfare administrators, immigration officers, economic regulators, and officers who award subsidies. The central question is: How can the quality of discretionary justice administered by such officers be improved?

The inquiry is not into the question of what is justice; instead, we assume that each reader has his own conception of justice, and we concentrate on the discretionary aspect of discretionary justice. Do the officers have too much or too little discretionary power, and what are the controls on that power? Our subject is justice for particular parties—not the much more discussed social justice, which deals with segments of a population. Our concern is limited to fairness in the exercise of discretionary power of governmental officers; it does not include problems of fairness in the manner in which one private party treats another private party. Our emphasis tends to be much more on injustice than on justice, for the areas of injustice provide the best opportunities for improving the quality of justice.

A half-dozen illustrations will show types of injustice that are now prevalent and can be reduced.

1. A, fourteen years old, throws a rock that breaks a wind-

shield. A policeman, who knows A's prominent father, cautions A and lets him go. B, also fourteen, commits the same act, and the same policeman arrests B, who is then convicted and punished. B has no prominent father.

2. Big Company pollutes a stream. Its lawyers and lobbyists quietly persuade the enforcement officers not to investigate. Little Company, having lawyers but not lobbyists, is investigated and prosecuted for polluting the stream to a lesser degree.

3. A welfare claimant is denied benefits to which she is entitled because an indolent administrator seeks to avoid the paperwork that must be done if the benefits are granted. The claimant is ignorant of her rights and meekly accepts the decision.

4. C and D are bank tellers, and both embezzle a small amount. The prosecutor brings a prosecution against C, who is 31, but not against D, who is 27. The prosecutor's reason is his secret rule of thumb: to be lenient with any first offender who is under 30. C is convicted and D goes free. Yet the further facts about the lives of C and D would lead a sentencing judge to give D a heavier penalty than C.

5. The X Company, a large corporation, learns that its principal competitor, the Y Company, which is still larger, is receiving a huge subsidy from the government which X believes Y is not legally entitled to receive. The subsidy gives Y a great advantage in price competition with X, and X's business is dwindling. Under the applicable law, X has no standing to challenge the legality of the subsidy in a reviewing tribunal.

6. Two aliens apply for permanent residence in a country. The officials have broad discretionary power and are slipshod in exercising it. They admit the one who is less qualified and exclude the one who is better qualified. The excluded alien has a theoretical remedy, but pursuing it is too expensive for his limited means.

The first step in our inquiry into how to improve the quality of discretionary justice is to locate the main clusters of injustice in our governmental and legal systems. Those clusters are clearly not in the highest courts of either the United States or any of the five European countries included in this study—Denmark,

France, Germany, Italy, and the Netherlands. Indeed, the clusters of injustice are not in any of the courts of the six countries, the main exception probably being the criminal courts of the large cities of the United States. The courts systematically find facts and apply previously existing law; such injustice as may be thought to result is in the nature of imperfection of the human beings who apply the law to the facts, not the product of basic inadequacy of the system. By and large, the same is true of administrative action based on systematic fact-finding and application of previously existing law.

The largest clusters of injustice in all six countries lie in the administrative application of governmental power in the absence of systematic fact-finding and beyond the reach of previously existing law that controls the result. In other words, the most injustice in the exercise of governmental power in cases involving identified parties probably occurs when officers who are not judges exercise unreviewed discretionary power without the kind of procedural protections that courts customarily provide. These essays focus on such discretionary power.

In my 1969 book, *Discretionary Justice,* dealing with discretion of American administrators, I wrote one sentence that now seems to deserve repetition with even greater emphasis: "The strongest need and the greatest promise for improving the quality of justice to individual parties in the entire legal and governmental system are in the areas where decisions necessarily depend more upon discretion than upon rules and principles and where formal hearings and judicial review are mostly irrelevant." On the basis of the limited samples we have taken of European discretionary justice, I believe that remark probably applies about equally to the European countries from which our samples have been taken.

The promise for improving the quality of justice is surely greatest in the areas where injustice is clustered; those areas, in the language of American administrative law, are the ones involving informal and unreviewed discretionary power. "Informal" means procedure not resembling that of the courtroom. "Unreviewed" means lack of a check by a superior authority, whether or not a superior authority has power to check. "Discretionary power" means power to make a choice: an officer has discretion whenever the effective limits on his power leave him free to make a choice among possible courses of action or inaction. What matters is not what procedure is authorized, but what is *in fact* used; not what is reviewable according to the applicable law, but what is *in fact* reviewed; not what limits the law places on the officer's discretionary power, but what limits are effective *in fact* in the particular case.

THE BACKGROUND

My opinion has long been that American and English literature of jurisprudence, public administration, and administrative law has been woefully inadequate on the subject of discretionary justice. Jurisprudence in the English language—including a good deal translated from other languages—has been too much concerned with judges and legislators and not enough with administrators, executives, police, and prosecutors. Jurisprudence acknowledges the law-discretion dichotomy and then spends itself almost entirely on the law half. We need a jurisprudence that will encompass all of justice, not just the easy half of it; we need a jurisprudence that will penetrate discretionary justice, as it has penetrated nondiscretionary justice.

The main task of the literature of public administration is to consider how to get the governmental job done, not how to improve the quality of justice that is administered in the process of doing that job. Public administration focuses on problems of organizing and managing staffs of employees, but it does not get down into the discretionary tasks of individual employees. In my inquiry into discretionary justice, I have been able to extract very little from the literature of public administration. American writers on public administration have been trying to develop a value-free science of administration, and that effort has diverted them from the needed processes of describing and criticizing what administrators do.

The literature of administrative law has been only peripherally helpful to a study of discretionary justice. Over the last three or four decades, American and English administrative law has been devoted to the 10 or 20 percent of the administrative process that involves either formal proceedings or judicial review, and it has almost completely neglected the 80 or 90 percent that involves informal and unreviewed action. That has been changing somewhat during the past five years, and I am immensely pleased to say that from half to two-thirds of the studies sponsored by the Administrative Conference of the United States, the official organ of the government to study the administrative process, have dealt significantly with problems of discretionary justice. The work of the Conference began as recently as 1968.

The initial reaction of most European lawyers to what I am saying is something like this: "We are as much concerned about injustice in administration as you are, and we have developed an effective system for correcting such injustice. That is one of the main functions of our administrative courts. One who is unfairly treated by a bureaucrat can take his case to an administrative court, where he gets an impartial determination. We have elaborate law that governs review of administrative action by administrative courts." I agree with much of that usual response. The administrative courts are very effective in protecting against injustice and in correcting injustice, and the elaborate law that guides or controls them is probably one of the greatest accomplishments in the world's legal systems.

But a further word needs to be spoken about administrative courts—a very important word that is seldom uttered in European legal circles. European law and legal literature are focused on the injustice that administrative courts correct, not on the injustice that administrative courts fail to correct. Where are the studies of administrative action that never or seldom comes before administrative courts? What portion of all administrative action is *in fact* unreviewable by an administrative court? Might that portion be as high as half?

If administrative decisions in a particular country are in the millions but decisions of the administrative court are in the hundreds or thousands, and if the decisions of the administrative court have little or no effect upon administrative practices in cases other than the ones that go to the administrative court, does justice or injustice depend almost entirely upon what administrators do and very little upon what administrative courts decide? If justice is to be done in the great bulk of administrative decisions, does it not have to be done by the administrators who make the initial decision in each case? Where is the European law that controls such initial decisions?

In my four-volume treatise on American administrative law, almost two-thirds of the discussion is devoted to the law that controls procedure for the initial action of administrators. Almost all of that law of administrative procedure is the product of judicial or legislative invention during the last half-century. European treatises on administrative law contain no substantial counterpart of the American procedural law controlling the initial action of administrators; yet some such law is beginning to develop and may soon become important. Those beginnings seem to me to deserve encouragement.

As an illustration of my observation that European administrative courts are effective in the business they handle, but that much administrative action that may involve injustice does not become a part of that business, let me point to the essay "Tax Relief Contracts in France." Since 1938, discretionary decisions involving many billions of francs have been made by the Ministry of Finance, with virtually no review by the Conseil d'Etat. Two or three cases have reached the Conseil from that program, involving only peripheral problems, not central or vital ones. The only decision of the Conseil that could control administrators significantly is one that the administrators must state reasons to the Conseil to justify a decision; the requirement is not that reasons must be given to the disappointed party in the more than 99.9 percent that do not go to the Conseil. I believe that justice or injustice in administering the program of tax relief contracts in France depends almost entirely on what the officials of the Ministry of Finance do, and hardly at all on protection afforded by the Conseil d'Etat. Of course, this one program is not necessarily typical of all European programs, but I believe that it is somewhat representative.

Another way to support my important observation that many types of administrative decisions are affected little, if at all, by the protections afforded by administrative courts is by pointing to the half-dozen illustrations of administrative injustice set forth in my preceding section. Let us examine each one from a different angle.

1. The policeman arrests one boy but not the other, and equal justice is clearly denied. The boy who is convicted has no legal remedy, either in the administrative court or in the criminal court. He is guilty, and the policeman's failure to arrest the other boy is no defense. The unequal justice is uncorrected by any reviewing authority outside the police organization.

2. Little Company has no tribunal to turn to for protection against a lawful investigation of its pollution, even though the unfairness of investigating its pollution and not that of Big Company is obvious.

3. The welfare claimant who meekly accepts an unlawful and unjust decision has a theoretical remedy but not a real one. The protections of an administrative court are inoperative in many such cases.

4. When one bank embezzler is prosecuted and the other goes free, no reviewing authority will correct the injustice to the one who is prosecuted.

5. Administrative courts and other courts generally deny standing to one corporation to challenge an unlawful award of a subsidy to a competitor. The injustice at the hands of the subsidy administrators goes uncorrected. (Apparently the German administrative court has recently allowed standing.)

6. The alien who is wrongfully excluded has a remedy in an administrative court, but pursuing it is too expensive for his limited means. Such a circumstance is one reason why justice often has to be done in the first instance if it is to be done at all. After all, probably only 1 or 2 percent of administrative determinations are in fact reviewed by administrative courts.

The present European administrative law seems to me exceedingly good, as far as it goes. But, like American administrative law, it has not yet sufficiently penetrated the areas of informal and unreviewed discretionary action, where the quality of justice is often lower than it is in the rest of our various legal systems.

The weak spots go back to the intrinsic nature of the human being. Unguided and uncontrolled discretionary power is exceedingly damaging to justice. The reason I am searching for ways to eliminate unnecessary discretion and to control necessary discretion is *not* that human beings cannot exercise unlimited and unguided discretion wisely, justly, and beneficently. Many can. Many do. The reason is that we do not know how to select the ones who can and do; most of our European and American and other administrators *in fact* exercise discretion wisely, justly, and beneficently only a part of the time. Out of a thousand officers, no matter how well screened, a large portion may be expected to abuse their discretionary power to a considerable extent, and some—perhaps only a few—are likely to engage in occasional abuse of power that is quite serious. This statement about the basic nature of the human being does not seem to me controversial; thoughtful people everywhere readily confirm it from their own observation and experience. Of course, everyone who lives among people has a foundation for making his own determination.

Many judges in Europe and America have unblemished integrity and thoroughly sound judgment and can therefore safely be trusted with a good deal of unguided discretionary power, but I think the planners of our system have nevertheless been wise to invent many ways to confine, structure, and check the discretionary power of our judges, because human weaknesses and inadequacies are sometimes perceptible in some judges.

The reason that so little effort has gone into finding ways to minimize discretionary injustice from administrators is not a belief that the injustice is insignificant; it is that finding ways to prevent or cure the injustice is so baffling. Such effort in America is limited to the last few years, and it seems to be limited in Europe to highly abstract writing. During the summer of 1970 I consulted a good many professors in leading European universities, asking each one what literature exists in his language that treats discretionary justice on the basis of investigations of administrative action within the ministries. I sought professors who were most likely to be informed, but everyone I consulted gave me the same answer—that nothing of that kind exists in his language, so far as he knows. A good many were aware of abstract writing about discretionary power, such as Jean-Claude Venezia's *Le Pouvoir Discrétionnaire* (1959) and Veli Merikoski's *Le Pouvoir Discrétionnaire de l'Administration* (1958). Both of these books refer to other writings in the same vein, but such literature has little in common with thinking that is based on factual investigation. German writers provide many abstract discussions of "ermessen," but not on a basis of empirical investigation. In France and the Netherlands I learned of studies of administration by sociologists, involving interviews in ministries, but the focus was efficiency, not the quality of justice. Here and there writings on special subjects, such as welfare administration or land control, deal incidentally with discretionary determinations, but nothing I have found deals systematically with that subject. In Germany, one leading professor seemed to speak with confidence when he went beyond the usual statement that he knew of nothing of the kind I was searching for; he stated that nothing of that kind has been written in the German language in the last fifty years. Of course, since my search has been neither systematic nor thorough, some study might exist that was not brought out by my interviews with professors.

If my impression is correct that no empirical research has been done in Europe on discretionary justice, then one of my hopes is that the present study, limited as it is, may lead the way for further research. The subject calls for a good deal of down-to-earth investigation of governmental practices and processes, and it calls for some jurisprudential thinking that is based on such investigation. The present study is tiny in comparison with what needs to be done, but it is at least a beginning.

THE OBJECTIVES

In my study of discretionary justice in America, based on many interviews, I have found that discretionary power is indispensable to modern government and that the cure for discretionary injustice cannot be the elimination of such power. But I have also found that all levels of American government—federal, state, and local—are shot through with *unnecessary* discretionary power, and I concluded that "we can and should cut back huge quantities of unnecessary discretionary power." I also found that we can do much more to control necessary discretionary power, and most of what I have written involves exploration of potentialities for developing better control.

I wondered whether Europeans know what Americans do not know—how to avoid the growth of unnecessary discretionary power, and how to control necessary discretionary power. A comparison of the powers and practices of German and American prosecutors led me to develop a hypothesis that they do: a German prosecutor has no discretionary power to withhold prosecution when the evidence that the defendant has committed a serious crime is reasonably clear and the law is not in doubt; yet an American prosecutor has unconfined, unstructured, and unchecked discretionary power to withhold prosecution in most such cases. Even when a German prosecutor exercises discretion, as he often does with respect to prosecuting for minor crimes, his discretion is tightly controlled, in contrast with the virtually complete lack of control of the American prosecutor's discretion with respect to prosecution for minor crimes. The contrast between the German and the American prosecutor, I thought, might mean that Europeans have a special understanding of discretion that Americans lack.

Alexander Pekelis, with a European background, had examined in depth both European and American legal institutions, and had written in his brilliant book, *Law and Social Action* (1950), that "comparative investigations thus far seem to reveal that in the administration of justice the common-law countries have traditionally relied upon a wide exercise of discretionary power to an incomparably greater extent than any civil-law country in Europe" (p. 83).

If Pekelis is right, how do the Europeans do it? What do they understand that the Americans do not understand? These questions seemed worth pursuing. But how? The search for literature turned up nothing significant, except some abstract writing that seemed to have little relation to reality. Those I consulted in European universities could not answer my questions.

On that basis, this inquiry was conceived. With the help of senior European professors, I selected some young faculty members—usually assistants (some of whom have since become professors)—and together we identified narrow subjects as samples of what Europeans do about discretionary power in various contexts.

The countries, places, people, and specific subjects were somewhat unsystematically chosen, to a large extent on the basis of such fortuities as who happened to be available and what his interests happened to be. My broad purpose was to take random samples of European discretionary power, to try to get a plurality of countries and a diversity of subjects, to keep each project rather small so that a thorough study could be made, to encourage each investigator not only to make findings but also to make judgments about the arrangements concerning discretionary power, and then, at the end, to try to put together the findings and ideas.

Each investigation was guided by a memorandum of mine entitled "Some General Guides for Research on Discretionary Justice," which lists and explains twenty particular inquiries that should be made on each subject, and by another memorandum of mine entitled "Samples of the Type of Questions That Should Be Considered in a Study of Discretion in the Administration of the German Statute against Water Pollution." The second memorandum contained fifty specific questions, but explained that the questions "are not the questions that should be studied; they are samples of *the type* of questions that might be considered." The water pollution study was started and never completed, but the questions prepared for it were a guide for all the studies.

As the inquiry progressed, the objectives seemed to broaden somewhat into a comparison of European and American systems for limiting and controlling discretionary power in governmental administration. The two major conclusions stated in the final chapter are wholly of that character. Lack of support for the hypothesis became clear at an early time, but we continued the inquiry into comparative European and American methods of limiting and controlling discretionary power.

THE METHOD

The main research method was interviewing of government administrators. We simply went to them to ask what they are doing, how they are doing it, with what successes and failures, and what ideas they have about how to do it better. An exceedingly important observation about interviews as a tool for making this kind of study is that they can be designed not merely to find facts about practices and processes but also to develop ideas. In our interviews we sought both facts and ideas—and mixtures of the two. I am convinced that interviews at their best can produce an interplay of two minds that penetrates intellectual territory which a single mind, operating alone, can seldom reach.

Perhaps I should mention in passing that we sometimes examined files. One of our investigators preferred that method over interviewing, and his study is a good one, but I think his work would have been more efficient if he had relied more heavily on interviews. We studied some small corners of our subject by using published reports of cases decided by administrative courts or other courts. Problems about discretion do sometimes reach reviewing authorities, whose decisions are reported. Indeed, some slight beginnings of law about discretionary justice can be found; they are discussed below, especially in the essay "Tax Relief Contracts in France," in my comments following that essay, and in the final chapter. But the treatments of discretionary justice by reviewing tribunals in reported opinions are no more than fragmentary. The only way to get an understanding of what administrators are doing and how they are doing it is by interviewing them and examining their files. That is what we have done.

Because I deem the method of interviewing so vital, and because that method seems underdeveloped in Europe, I shall set forth my experience and ideas about interviewing, even at the expense of seeming somewhat anecdotal.

I first talked with government administrators in West Virginia in 1937 and 1938, when I was trying to develop an understanding of American administrative law and was curious about questions that local administrators could answer. Then I became a member of the staff of the Attorney General's Committee on Administrative Procedure and spent a full year in Washington, 1939–40, interviewing administrators and writing reports describing and criticizing the practices. Perhaps over a period of nearly forty years I have spent the equivalent of more than four years of full-time work in interviewing administrators of federal, state, and local governments.

During 1960 I spent four months in London for the purpose of interviewing in the ministries, especially in the Ministry of Housing and Local Government and in the Home Office. Friends in British universities warned me that interviewing in the ministries would be impossible. When I listened to a public lecture by a professor on institutional administrative decisions and could not understand some abstract portions of the lecture, I asked the professor afterward why he did not use concrete illustrations from actual experience in the ministries. He replied that such experience is unavailable. I asked: "Then why don't you go to the administrators and get the information by interviewing them?" He replied: "That isn't done. You can't go into the ministries to interview!" Another senior professor in friendly and fatherly fashion explained to me that interviewing would be impossible. I asked why. He said it would be improper, that professors in England all know it would be improper, and that administrators would not be willing to talk to outsiders. I asked why, in a democracy, anyone should not be allowed to talk with those who administer the government. He insisted that it could not be done. His view was corroborated by others present. They all seemed to think that the outlander from America had raised an outlandish question.

I found that interviewing in the ministries in London was no more difficult than interviewing in executive departments in Washington. Although at first I arranged introductions and appointments, I soon found that unnecessary. I could go to a building, look at the directory in the entrance hall, select an administrator, go to his office, introduce myself, explain that I had questions to ask, get him interested in the questions, be given information on almost any subject not properly considered confidential, develop some interplay of minds, and even be invited back for further sessions.

That London experience was largely the basis for the present project. Those I talked with in the various continental countries usually expressed the opinion that interviewing could not be done in the ministries, and each collaborator with whom I arranged for a study expressed doubts and reluctance about interviewing. In one instance, when my European collaborator seemed unwilling to start interviewing, I insisted that he arrange an interview for me and then accompany me to serve as interpreter; I had to demonstrate to him that an administrator would permit such interviews. The interview went smoothly; we learned about as much as could be learned in the time spent. The officer who was interviewed was no more reluctant to help in a scholarly project than his counterpart in America would have been. My colleague was convinced, and thereafter he did a good deal of interviewing with successful results.

What I am saying about the general European assumption that interviewing of governmental administrators is either impossible or improper seems exceedingly important. The usual assumption is plainly unsound, as our experience has shown.

The usual European reluctance about interviewing in government offices may partly account for the fact that European thinking about administrative action tends to be much more abstract than American thinking. Books and articles often show this. I have been acutely aware of this difference in my relations with my European collaborators. At times I have been pushed toward the exaggerated conclusion that a European scholar, in order to report and analyze ten pages of factual materials, must first write a fifty-page theoretical introduction.

Of course, I favor theory and abstract thinking, but I think that laying the factual foundation should usually come first, even though something in the nature of theory is indispensable to knowing what facts to go after. Developing theory and finding facts can move forward together, interacting with each other at all stages of an inquiry. In this project I have tried to do all I can to minimize the advance theorizing and then to limit the theorizing to what can be solidly built on a factual foundation.

Our method, then, has a half-dozen ingredients: (1) on the basis of our general European and American knowledge, identifying problems about discretion that seem worthy of study by throwing European light on them; (2) using interviews with administrators, and to a much lesser extent inspection of files, as tools for locating problems about the exercise of discretionary power and the control of such power; (3) describing our findings, and freely intermixing criticisms and ideas with the descriptions; (4) as far as feasible, trying to refrain from theorizing until a proper factual foundation has been laid; (5) continually comparing European experience and ideas with American experience and ideas; (6) unabashedly using subjective judgment in producing a mixture of findings and ideas, with an emphasis upon ideas, and without pretending that the mixture resembles pure science.

CHAPTER TWO

The German Prosecutor

JOACHIM HERRMANN

Kenneth Culp Davis has remarked that Americans may have considerable difficulty imagining a criminal justice system based on the concept that the prosecuting authority should have limited, rather than pervasive and uncontrolled, discretionary powers.[1] A system of this kind does, however, exist. Prosecuting attorneys in West Germany are required, except in certain situations specified in the codes and statutes, to prosecute all charges for which there is sufficient evidence to justify a conviction.[2] The German prosecutor is not without discretion; the scope of his discretion has increased steadily and is still growing. Unlike the American situation, however, the discretion of the prosecutor in this system is strictly limited by the Code of Criminal Procedure; it is guided by statutory standards and, to a certain extent, is controlled by the courts.

The striking difference between the two systems reasonably causes Americans to wonder how the German prosecutor manages to do his job, despite this restricted discretion, in a way that seems to be accepted by the public. There is no quick and simple answer; various social, political, and legal factors must be taken into consideration. If an inquiry were initially directed to the question of how prosecuting attorneys make practical use

The examples of the actual exercise of discretion contained in this chapter are based on interviews with prosecutors, defense attorneys, and judges in Freiburg, Munich, and Augsburg. Without their cooperation the research would not have been possible.

1. K. DAVIS, DISCRETIONARY JUSTICE: A PRELIMINARY INQUIRY 191–92 (1971).

2. The duty is stated in § 152(2) of the West German Code of Criminal Procedure: "Except as otherwise provided by law, it [i.e., the prosecution] is obligated to take action in case of all acts which are punishable by a court and

of their discretionary powers, we could gain only limited insights into the working of the German system. It is more helpful to begin by explaining the origin of the idea of compulsory prosecution in the German system and why it is today considered the fundamental principle governing the prosecutor's activities. This article will also briefly show, by examining the German Penal Code, that problems solved by the wide discretion of the American prosecutor do not exist, or are solved by other means, in Germany. Only then can the discussion meaningfully turn to its main focus, an investigation of the extent of the prosecutor's discretion, its limits, and its pattern, both in theory and in practice.

THE DEVELOPMENT OF THE CONCEPT OF COMPULSORY PROSECUTION

The office of the prosecutor was created in the German states in the middle of the nineteenth century by splitting the investigative and judicial functions of the inquisitorial judge. The investigative function was entrusted to a separate official, the prosecutor.[3] Some states, particularly in the South, decided that the prosecutor should be legally bound to prosecute a charge whenever there was sufficient evidence to obtain a conviction; other states, including Prussia, gave broad discretionary powers to the prosecutor.[4] The Code of Criminal Procedure of the German Reich was enacted in 1877 and, with numerous re-

---

capable of prosecution, so far as there is a sufficient factual basis." An English translation of the Code is published in 10 AMERICAN SERIES OF FOREIGN PENAL CODES: THE GERMAN CODE OF CRIMINAL PROCEDURE (H. Niebler transl. 1965) [hereafter cited as 10 FOREIGN PENAL CODES].

    The German prosecutorial system recently has come under much discussion. See K. DAVIS, *supra* note 1, at 193–95; Jescheck, *The Discretionary Powers of the Prosecuting Attorney in West Germany*, 18 AM. J. COMP. L. 508 (1970); Schmidt, *Introduction* to CODE OF CRIMINAL PROCEDURE, 10 FOREIGN PENAL CODES, *supra*, at 10; Schram, *The Obligation to Prosecute in West Germany*, 17 AM. J. COMP. L. 627 (1969). *See also* FOREIGN OFFICE, 2 MANUAL OF GERMAN LAW 140 (1952); Williams, *Discretion in Prosecuting*, 1956 CRIM. L. REV. 222; Wolff, *Criminal Justice in Germany* (pt. 1), 42 MICH. L. REV. 1067, 1077–78 (1944).

    3. *See* Langbein, *Controlling Prosecutorial Discretion in Germany*, 41 U. CHI. L. REV. 439 (1974); Wagner, *Der objektive Staatsanwalt—Idee und Wirklichkeit*, 1974 JURISTENZEITUNG 212.

    4. *See* E. SCHMIDT, EINFÜHRUNG IN DIE GESCHICHTE DER DEUTSCHEN STRAFRECHTS-

visions, is still in effect in Germany. The Code adopted the idea of compulsory prosecution; equal enforcement of the criminal law and protection against prosecutorial arbitrariness were deemed predominant values.

Although the power to prosecute crimes in Germany was separated from the inquisitorial judge, it continued to be entrusted to the judicial branch, under the authority of the Minister of Justice.[5] The prosecutor, therefore, does not act as an administrator trying to attain practical goals; instead, his function is limited to the judicial task of applying the provisions of the Penal Code to the facts of each case.

Compulsory prosecution, except where otherwise provided by law, is regarded as a German constitutional requirement based on the equal rights clause.[6] In addition, the German constitutional concept of the rule of law does not permit broad discretionary power. It is feared that vast discretion would result in local differences in the administration of criminal law and subject the prosecutor to the suspicion that he might be influenced by political motives and considerations of expediency.[7]

Citizens are protected against unjust convictions and oppressive punishment by the Penal Code, rather than by individual prosecuting attorneys. This situation is a result of the nineteenth-century constitutional movement on the European Continent, which was aimed at limiting the absolute power of the monarch and his administration, and which opposed all deprivations of life, liberty, and property that were not legislatively approved. While the courts in the United States were designed to protect citizens' rights against improper infringement by the

PFLEGE 330–31 (3d ed. 1965); Schram, *supra* note 2, at 627; Wagner, *Zum Legalitätsprinzip,* in FESTSCHRIFT FÜR DEN 45. DEUTSCHEN JURISTENTAG 149, 151–60 (1964).

5. K. DAVIS, *supra* note 1, at 194–95; K. PETERS, STRAFPROZESS 139–40 (2d ed. 1966); E. SCHMIDT, *supra* note 4, at 331; Jescheck, *supra* note 2, at 509. *See also* West German Court Organization Act §§ 141–52. A translation of the sections is included in 10 FOREIGN PENAL CODES, *supra* note 2, at 214–15.

6. Wagner, *supra* note 4, at 173; Faller, *Verfassungsrechtliche Grenzen des Opportunitätsprinzips im Strafprozess,* in FESTGABE FÜR THEODOR MAUNZ 69, 77–82 (1971).

7. H. HENKEL, STRAFVERFAHRENSRECHT 96 (2d ed. 1968); E. KERN & C. ROXIN, STRAFVERFAHRENSRECHT 59 (11th ed. 1972); K. PETERS, *supra* note 5, at 144; Jescheck, *supra* note 2, at 511; Schram, *supra* note 2, at 627; Wagner, *supra* note 4, at 159–60.

government, the Europeans delegated this task to the legislature. Today in the United States, court-created procedural and evidentiary safeguards provide protection against improper governmental action; in Europe such protection is considered to be the province of the written statute. Thus there is general agreement in Germany that it is better to amend the Penal Code than to alter the policies of the prosecutor, if the administration of the criminal law produces undesired results.[8]

This concept presupposes a penal code designed to state general principles of responsibility and to include comprehensive, carefully framed, and abstract definitions of offenses and sanctions that are accepted by the general public. The extent to which the German Penal Code meets these requirements can be investigated by examining some examples.

PROSECUTORIAL DISCRETION AND THE PENAL CODE

Extensive Judicial Interpretation of Criminal Law

The German Penal Code defines most offenses in more general and abstract terms than typical American criminal codes. As a result German judges often engage in a great deal of statutory construction—for example, when the definition of an offense appears to be so wide as to include conduct not regarded as criminal. Strict construction of penal statutes was never accepted in German law, because it was incompatible with the Code's abstract definitions of crimes.

One example of extensive construction is the interpretation of the provision on breach of trust.[9] The literal wording of the Code makes it a crime to neglect the duty to manage properly another person's property interests so as to cause damage to them. This provision is too broad, since it covers a simple

8. Wagner, *supra* note 4, at 159; Baumann, *Über die notwendigen Veränderungen im Bereich des Vermögensschutzes*, 1972 JURISTENZEITUNG 1, 3–6; Peters, *Die Begrenzung des Strafrechts bei zivilrechtlichen Verhältnissen als materiellsrechtliches und prozessuales Problem*, in FESTSCHRIFT FÜR EBERHARD SCHMIDT 488 (1961); Heinitz, *Zweifelsfragen des Opportunitätsprinzips*, in FESTSCHRIFT FÜR THEODOR RITTLER 327, 335 (1957).

9. Penal Code § 266. An English translation of the Code is published in 4 AMERICAN SERIES OF FOREIGN PENAL CODES: THE GERMAN PENAL CODE (G. Mueller & T. Buergenthal transl. 1961).

breach of contract and other activities that obviously should not be called criminal. The courts have therefore defined the meaning of "managing property interests" to include only activities of some importance and independence, where the person concerned is given significant liberty of action and responsibility.[10]

The prohibition against leaving the scene of a traffic accident [11] has similarly been judicially restricted. This section forbids people who have been involved in a traffic accident from fleeing to try to avoid identification. The German High Federal Court of Appeals has held that the provision does not apply to a driver of a car who has caused damage only to himself; the court said the purpose of the law is to help injured parties in collecting evidence for a claim of damages, not to aid criminal investigations.[12] Further, commentators agree that a driver who causes trivial damages to a parked, unoccupied car is not required to remain at the scene of the accident if he leaves his name and address.[13]

Another instance of judicial narrowing of the Penal Code involves the law of defamation.[14] Although there is no basis for such an exception in the statutory language, defamatory remarks made to a third person are not punished if made among family members or close friends.[15] Similarly, the provision on abandonment is too broad; it includes anyone who abandons a person charged to his care who is helpless because of youth, infirmity, or illness.[16] Parents who leave their small children alone in the house for an evening would be guilty of an offense for which

10. Decisions of the High Court of Appeals of the German Reich [REICHSGERICHT, hereafter RGSt]: 71 RGSt 90 (1937); 69 RGSt 279 (1935). Decisions of the High Federal Court of Appeals of the Federal Republic of Germany [BUNDESGERICHTS-HOF, hereafter BGHSt]: 1 BGHSt 186 (1951); 4 BGHSt 170 (1953). *See also* R. MAURACH, DEUTSCHES STRAFRECHT, BESONDERER TEIL 343–45 (5th ed. 1969).

11. Penal Code § 142.

12. 8 BGHSt 263 (1955).

13. R. MAURACH, *supra* note 10, at 716; A. SCHÖNKE & H. SCHRÖDER, STRAFGESETZ-BUCH, § 142, annot. No. 35 (16th ed. 1972). Where the damage is not trivial, the length of time a driver must wait for other parties to show up is not fixed by the Code, but depends upon the facts of each case. R. MAURACH, *supra* note 10, at 716; A. SCHÖNKE & H. SCHRÖDER, *supra*, annot. Nos. 33–38.

14. Penal Code §§ 185 *et seq.*

15. R. MAURACH, *supra* note 10, at 138–39; A. SCHÖNKE & H. SCHRÖDER, *supra* note 13, § 185, annot. No. 8.

16. Penal Code § 221.

they could be sentenced to imprisonment for not less than three months. It is generally agreed that this section is violated only if the abandonment endangers the victim's life or limb.[17]

These examples show that German law relies on careful and elaborate judicial interpretation of the substantive law to solve problems that the United States often leaves to the discretion of the prosecutor. Judicial interpretation of substantive law is successful, however, only if the definitions meet certain minimum requirements. For example, in the 1950s the German Penal Code defined some of the political offenses by extremely vague terms. The Federal Attorney General in charge of prosecuting the more serious political offenses argued that the substantive law of political crimes could not be reconciled with the rule of compulsory prosecution. He stated that the sweeping definitions of the Penal Code necessitated broad discretionary power for the prosecuting attorney.[18]

The doctrine of extensive judicial construction is also used to broaden the definition of an offense if the interests of justice so require. For instance, in the provision on dangerous assault, "by means of a weapon" is interpreted to include the throwing of hydrochloric acid into the victim's face [19] and the setting of a dog.[20] In the definition of robbery, "by force" includes nonviolent narcotization of the victim.[21]

The abstract definitions in the Code obviously create the potential for a good deal of prosecutorial discretion. Prosecutors are, however, usually hesitant to take advantage of this discretionary power by deciding doubtful cases themselves. In close cases they prefer to prosecute and leave to the judiciary the function of deciding open questions and clarifying the definitions of offenses.[22] The German High Federal Court of Appeals has stated this principle more forcefully; it held that prosecutors must strictly follow the court's decisions in interpreting the

---

17. 21 BGHSt 44 (1966); R. MAURACH, *supra* note 10, at 48.

18. M. GÜDE, PROBLEME DES POLITISCHEN STRAFRECHTS 23 (1957). *See also* Schram, *supra* note 2, at 631.

19. Penal Code § 223a. 1 BGHSt 1 (1950).

20. 14 BGHSt 152 (1960).

21. Penal Code § 249; 1 BGHSt 145 (1951). *See also* S. KADISH & M. PAULSEN, CRIMINAL LAW AND ITS PROCESSES 46 (2d ed. 1969).

22. *See* K. DAVIS, *supra* note 1, at 194.

Code.[23] This statement was surprising because, in civil law countries, court decisions are regarded not as sources but as interpretations of the law. Accordingly, the holding of the High Federal Court of Appeals was widely repudiated.[24] It was said that the idea of compulsory prosecution cannot be taken to exclude the prosecutors' right to interpret the law, since they function as an independent agency of the judiciary. The extent to which they actually exercise this right is another question.

Lenient Sentencing Policy

Another factor favoring limited prosecutorial discretion is that sentences in Germany are considerably less severe than in the United States. Professor Zeisel, who is familiar with the criminal law systems in both countries, has suggested that a one-month prison sentence may be imposed in European countries for crimes that would result in imprisonment for one year in America.[25]

Mandatory minimum sentences provided in the German Penal Code are generally more lenient than in American codes. This fact is particularly true where a criminal defendant has previously been convicted of a crime. While a number of American states require lengthy imprisonment for recidivists,[26] German law sets the minimum at only six months for third convictions when the defendant has been in jail before and "failed to heed the warning of the prior sentences." [27] Only habitual criminals who have previously been convicted of serious crimes and twice have been imprisoned for a year may be placed in protective custody for an unlimited time if necessary for the safety of the community.[28] The differences in sentencing are even

23. 15 BGHSt 155 (1960).

24. *E.g.,* K. Peters, *supra* note 5, at 144–45; E. Kern & C. Roxin, *supra* note 7, at 44–45.

25. Zeisel, *Die Rolle der Geschworenen in den USA,* 21 Österreichische Juristenzeitung 121, 123 (1966). *See also* Clark, *The Courts, the Police and the Community,* 46 S. Cal. L. Rev. 1, 4 (1972).

26. ABA Project on Minimum Standards for Criminal Justice, Standards Relating to Sentencing Alternatives and Procedures 164 (1967); *The Habitual Criminal—A Comparative Study,* 13 McGill L. J. 652 (1967).

27. Penal Code § 17. German law on recidivism was changed in 1969; previously, there were several provisions dealing with recidivists. *See, e.g., id.* § 20a (dangerous habitual criminals); *id.* § 244 (repeated property offenses).

28. *Id.* § 42e. This provision was also changed in 1969.

more clearly demonstrated by the average sentencing practices in each country. In America, "[m]ore than one-half of the adult felony offenders sentenced to state prisons in 1960 were committed for maximum terms of 5 years or more; almost one-third were sentenced to terms of at least 10 years." [29] In Germany in 1970, over 60 percent of the prison sentences were for less than six months, and most of those sentences were suspended.[30]

German judges generally impose sentences that are close to the mandatory minimum.[31] The Penal Code also allows sentences below the minimum punishment for some serious offenses if mitigating circumstances are found.[32] Judges often reduce sentences not because such circumstances exist, but merely because a less severe sentence seems appropriate.[33]

Reduction of charges and plea bargaining in the United States, which would be impossible without wide prosecutorial discretion, are to a great extent intended to avoid excessively harsh sanctions. The problems created by the severe sentences in America do not exist in Germany, thus removing one reason to grant broad discretion to the prosecutor.

[margin note: Because sentences are short, prosecutors do not need discretion.]

INSTANCES OF PROSECUTORIAL DISCRETION

Compulsory prosecution is the general rule controlling the German prosecutor's activities whenever felonies and serious misdemeanors are involved.[34] Felonies such as murder, robbery, rape, perjury, and arson are prosecuted if there is sufficient evidence to prove the defendant's guilt. Compulsory prosecution in these cases is considered necessary because of the serious char-

29. PRESIDENTIAL COMMISSION ON LAW ENFORCEMENT AND THE ADMINISTRATION OF JUSTICE, TASK FORCE REPORT, THE COURTS, at 17 (1967).

30. H. JESCHECK, LEHRBUCH DES STRAFRECHTS—ALLGEMEINER TEIL 22 (2d ed. 1972).

31. K. ROLINSKI, DIE PRÄGNANZTENDENZ IM STRAFURTEIL 81 (1969); J. SCHIEL, UNTERSCHIEDE IN DER DEUTSCHEN STRAFRECHTSPRECHUNG 25–27 (1969). Except during the Nazi period, this tendency has steadily strengthened since the enactment of the Penal Code in 1871.

32. *See, e.g.,* Penal Code §§ 154 (perjury), 217 (infanticide), 228 (certain cases of assault), 249 (robbery).

33. F. EXNER, STUDIEN ÜBER DIE STRAFZUMESSUNGSPRAXIS DER DEUTSCHEN GERICHTE 20–23, 84–85 (1931); K. ROLINSKI, *supra* note 31, at 82; J. SCHIEL, *supra* note 31, at 24.

34. For a definition of the categories of crimes under the Penal Code, see text and note at note 77 *infra.*

acter of the offenses. German lawyers agree that the interests of justice, as well as deterrence, require equal prosecution of serious crimes.

The rule of compulsory prosecution sometimes leads to extreme consequences. In one case, a young man took two apples from a display outside a store; the storekeeper asked him to return the apples, and the young man resisted with force. The use of force to defend stolen goods is a felony under the German law. Thus the prosecutor had to file a charge, and the young man was convicted.[35] In another case, a police officer had collected fifteen German marks [36] for traffic fines on a Friday night. He spent the money during the weekend, but he intended to turn over fifteen marks when he reported to duty the following Tuesday; there was no doubt that he had sufficient means to do so. Nevertheless, the police officer was charged with and convicted of aggravated embezzlement in office. This offense is a felony, so the prosecutor was compelled to prosecute.[37]

Despite the strong emphasis placed on compulsory prosecution, the German prosecutor has always exercised certain types of discretion. The next part of this article will discuss the situations in which prosecutorial discretion exists.

The Power to Pass on the Sufficiency of the Evidence

The prosecutor will only bring a charge when he determines that sufficient evidence exists to obtain a conviction. Even when the rule of compulsory prosecution applies, he can close the case if he concludes that the evidence will probably not support a conviction.[38] In practice, most investigations are terminated

35. 3 BGHSt 76 (1952).

36. One German mark is currently worth about 40 American cents.

37. Decision of the High State Court of Appeals of Cologne, 1968 NEUE JURISTISCHE WOCHENSCHRIFT 2348. In the late 1920s, a public officer who had taken 20 German pennies was charged with simple theft in office (today 20 West German pennies would be equivalent to less than 10 American cents). Although the offense was only a misdemeanor, the prosecuting attorney did not use the fact that a small amount was involved to discontinue proceedings. He was apparently moved to prosecute because a public officer was involved. Decision of the Highest State Court of Appeals of Bavaria, 37 GOLTDAMMERS ARCHIV FÜR STRAFRECHT 130 (1927).

38. Code of Criminal Procedure § 170. *See also* K. DAVIS, *supra* note 1, at 194; E. SCHMIDT, LEHRKOMMENTAR ZUR STRAFPROZESSORDNUNG UND ZUM GERICHTSVERFASSUNGSGESETZ, TEIL I, 386 (2d ed. 1964); Jescheck, *supra* note 2, at 511.

in this way.[39] In doubtful cases, however, prosecutors generally hesitate to use this discretionary power. They realize that they are familiar with the case merely from the files, and a judge at the end of a trial will be in a better position to decide the defendant's guilt.

There are, however, exceptions to this general rule. A middle-aged man, who had a son in his early twenties from a former marriage, married a young girl. Son and stepmother had sexual relations, and the father reported them to the police. Until 1973, intercourse between in-laws was a crime according to German law; [40] the defendants had unquestionably committed the act, and ordinarily a charge would have been brought. The prosecuting attorney, who was known among his colleagues for his readiness to terminate investigations, questioned the two young people separately and asked whether they had known that their act was illegal. Both answered in the negative, and the prosecutor dropped the investigation for insufficiency of evidence. Under German law, they could have been convicted only upon proof that their ignorance of the law was avoidable.[41] The prosecutor did not, however, attempt to procure evidence that the young people could have known of the illegality of their conduct.

The prosecuting attorney who considers discontinuing an investigation frequently must decide whether further investigations will reveal additional evidence. This question is particularly important in cases of white-collar crimes involving complex business transactions, or where a minor crime has been only routinely investigated. Compulsory prosecution demands thorough investigation of every case, but the chances of

39. H. DAHS, HANDBUCH DES STRAFVERTEIDIGERS 154 (3d ed. 1971); K. PETERS, *supra* note 5, at 88. In 1971 in Bade-Württemberg, one of the West German states, prosecutors discontinued 50 percent of the proceedings because of insufficient evidence. Blankenburg, *Die Staatsanwaltschaft im Prozess sozialer Kontrolle,* 5 KRIMINOLOGISCHES JOURNAL 181, 182 (1973). The actual practice varies among the local offices. In Bade-Württemberg, for example, one office discontinued 61 percent of the proceedings for insufficient evidence, while another office did so in only 45 percent of its cases. Blankenburg, *id.* at 183. The comparison is somewhat distorted because of differences in record keeping.

40. Penal Code § 173 (incest).

41. *See* Ryu & Silving, *Error Juris: A Comparative Study,* 24 U. CHI. L. REV. 421, 448–58, 461–65 (1957).

finding new evidence must be carefully evaluated; it is obviously permissible for the prosecutor to avoid futile inquiries.

Citizen remedies for failure to prosecute.

A prosecuting attorney who knows that he has sufficient evidence for a charge, but fails to prosecute, can be charged with favoritism.[42] This law is intended to guarantee the operation of the rule of compulsory prosecution; prosecutions for favoritism are, however, quite rare.[43] With regard to police officers, also covered by the provision on favoritism, the German High Federal Court of Appeals has held that the duty to prosecute should not exceed the working capacity of the officer concerned.[44]

The prosecutor's decision not to investigate, or not to investigate further because of insufficient evidence or because there was no violation of law, is not necessarily the end of a case. The victim, if he has reported the crime, can file a formal complaint within a one-month period.[45] The attorney general, the chief prosecutor in the state,[46] reviews the prosecutor's decision by examining the file for that particular case; he is empowered to direct the prosecutor to reopen the investigation and file charges, but this action is rarely taken. Because of the availability of these procedures, the prosecutor seems to be somewhat more reluctant to discontinue an investigation when there is a victim who can bring such a complaint.

A victim whose formal complaint is rejected can file a motion with the highest state court of appeals, asking that the prosecuting attorney be directed to file a charge.[47] This judicial review is intended as a safeguard against prosecutorial abuse of power and is regarded as an important means for the citizen to enforce the rule of compulsory prosecution. The opportunity for judi-

42. Penal Code § 346.

43. German official statistics combine the offenses of favoritism, *id.* § 346, and permitting prisoners to escape, *id.* § 347. In 1970, for both offenses, a total of eight cases are reported. Four defendants were convicted, one was acquitted, and in three cases proceedings were terminated by the courts without a decision on the defendant's guilt. *See* STATISTISCHES BUNDESAMT, BEVÖLKERUNG UND KULTUR, REIHE 9: RECHTSPFLEGE 1970, 42 (1972).

44. 18 BGHSt 19 (1960).

45. For details of this procedure, see Jescheck, *supra* note 2, at 512 and Langbein, *supra* note 3, at 463–65.

46. The Federal Attorney General is responsible for prosecuting few cases involving political matters. *See* Jescheck, *supra* note 2, at 512.

47. Code of Criminal Procedure §§ 172–75.

cial review is rarely seized, partly because the victim must pay his legal fees and the court costs if his motion is denied.[48]

In addition to the formal complaint, the victim can also attack the prosecutor's decision to stop investigating a case by filing a departmental complaint.[49] The departmental complaint is directed to the prosecutor's superior and accuses the prosecutor who closed the case of malfeasance. The prosecutor must explain his reasons for terminating the investigation, and the superior's decision is based on the file maintained by the prosecutor. If the superior concludes that the prosecutor's decision was incorrect, the investigation is reopened. Departmental complaints are often filed, but they have been successful only in a few cases in which new evidence was introduced by the victim.

In practice, control over the prosecutor's decisions is exercised through close supervision and cooperation in the local prosecution office. The head of the local office and the supervisors of its various sections control the work of their subordinates by personal contacts and review of the files. Regular conferences are held to discuss individual cases and to work out general patterns for structuring prosecutorial discretion. To close any case, the prosecutor must obtain the approval of his superior. Above the local level, cooperation among prosecutors is less extensive; personal contacts are infrequent and meetings to discuss law enforcement problems rarely occur.

A prosecutor who has decided that the evidence in a case is sufficient to obtain a conviction cannot always prosecute. Some criminal offenses can be prosecuted only after the victim has filed a motion for prosecution.[50] These offenses involve primarily violations of personal interests, such as breach of domestic peace, defamation, seduction of a girl younger than sixteen, abduction of minors or females, causing bodily harm, domestic theft and fraud, unauthorized use of a vehicle, and damage to

48. *Id.* § 177.

49. For details of this procedure, see Jescheck, *supra* note 2, at 512 and Langbein, *supra* note 3, at 465–66.

50. FOREIGN OFFICE, *supra* note 2, at 94–95; Jescheck, *supra* note 2, at 514; Wolff, *supra* note 2, at 1078. The motion for prosecution must be filed within three months either with the police, the prosecutor's office, or a court. Penal Code § 61; Code of Criminal Procedure § 158. The three-month period begins when the victim learns of the offense and ascertains the identity of the offender.

property.[51] The victim in these cases is given an option to file a motion and have the offender prosecuted, or not file and thereby protect his personal affairs from the intrusion of a police investigation and the publicity of a trial.

Offenses Subject to Private Charge by the Victim

Another instance of prosecutorial discretion is found in connection with the victim's right to prefer a private charge.[52] The German Code of Criminal Procedure provides for private prosecution in cases of breaching domestic peace, insult, causing bodily harm, threatening with a serious crime, violating the secrecy of the mails, causing damage to property, and violating copyright laws and laws against unfair competition.[53] The common characteristic of these offenses is not their triviality, but the predominantly personal character of the interests involved. Thus the victim is permitted to assume the role of a prosecutor and bring the offender to trial; the procedural rules in private prosecutions are essentially the same as in public prosecutions.[54] As late as the 1950s private charges for cases involving insults were not unusual, but today they have become an exception.[55] Victims of an offense obviously prefer to report it to the police or to the prosecuting attorney in order to have their case investigated by public authorities.

The prosecutor is authorized to file a public charge in cases subject to private prosecution only if it is in the "public interest." [56] The meaning of the public interest requirement is

51. For some offenses, the victim may file a private charge. *See* text and notes at notes 52–61 *infra.* For certain offenses involving bodily harm, a "special public interest" in prosecution may replace the victim's motion. *See* text and notes at notes 62–67 *infra.*

52. FOREIGN OFFICE, *supra* note 2, at 154; Jescheck, *supra* note 2, at 513; Wolff, *supra* note 2, at 1077 n.23.

53. Code of Criminal Procedure § 374.

54. *See id.* §§ 374–94.

55. As to the former practice, see Wolff, *supra* note 2, at 1077 n.23. Today in one South German court district with 300,000 residents, there are approximately 50 private prosecutions per year.

56. Code of Criminal Procedure § 376. Where proceedings by the victim have been initiated, the prosecutor can assume control of the case, placing the victim in the position of an intervenor. *See id.* § 377; FOREIGN OFFICE, *supra* note 2, at 154.

explained in the Uniform Rules of Criminal Procedure.[57] Rule 76 states that generally the public interest is involved if the particular violation affected people in addition to the victim and if the prosecution is of public concern because of the severe, brutal, or dangerous character of the offense, the motives of the offender, or his position in public life.

Despite its vague language, Rule 76 has to some extent controlled prosecutorial discretion. For example, insignificant quarrels and fights among neighbors or insults exchanged by automobile drivers are ordinarily left to private prosecution. But when a former German Chancellor was publicly slapped in the face by a woman who disapproved of his activities during the Nazi period, a public charge was brought. Public prosecution was also initiated when a lawyer called a witness a shameless liar in open court and when a police officer insulted an automobile driver who, after being stopped for speeding, interfered with the checking of other vehicles.[58] Prosecutors generally do not take action in cases of minor bodily injuries caused within the family, but the public interest is deemed to require prosecution if a father terrorizes his family or a child is physically abused. Simple assaults during barroom brawls are not viewed as important enough to require a public charge; the decision would be different, however, if an organized gang molested diners in restaurants.

The offenses that can be prosecuted by private persons are also included in the group of crimes for which a public charge may be brought only upon the victim's motion. As a result, a prosecuting attorney who believes that the public interest requires a public prosecution cannot do anything if the motion is not filed.[59] The rule of compulsory prosecution is supplanted

57. These rules were administratively promulgated by the states to give guidelines for deciding technical procedural questions and to structure the exercise of prosecutorial discretion. They are not, however, legally binding. The text of the Rules is set forth in T. KLEINKNECHT, STRAFPROZESSORDNUNG, Appendix F 1, "Richtlinien für das Strafverfahren und das Bussgeldverfahren," 1525–1673 (31st ed. 1974). See also E. KERN & C. ROXIN, supra note 7, at 12.

58. See K. Homann, Der Begriff des "öffentlichen Interesses" in den §§ 376, 153 StPO und § 232 StGB at 70–72 (doctoral thesis, University of Göttingen, 1971).

59. In some cases involving bodily harm, a "special public interest" in prosecution may replace the victim's motion. See text and notes at notes 62–67 infra.

by the principle that the ultimate decision to prosecute in these cases should be made by the victim. If the prosecutor decides, however, that the public interest does not require public charges, the injured party has no right to appeal his decision. In some cases the victim has tried to persuade the prosecutor to assume control of the case, because public prosecution involves less effort and risk for a private citizen.[60] If the prosecutor is unwilling, the victim might file a departmental complaint, but such complaints are rarely successful.[61]

The Special Public Interest Requirement in Cases Involving Bodily Harm

In cases involving intentional infliction of bodily harm or negligently causing bodily harm,[62] public charges may be brought only upon motion by the victim, unless official intervention is deemed necessary by reason of "special public interest." [63] The requirement of "special" public interest is a stricter standard than the public interest standard applicable to offenses that are subject to private prosecution.[64] Again, the Uniform Rules of Criminal Procedure provide guidance for the prosecutor's discretionary determination.[65] A special interest in public prosecution exists if the offender was previously convicted of a similar crime, if he acted recklessly, or, in the case of a traffic accident, if the driver was under the influence of alcohol or caused serious harm. The prosecutor should also consider whether the victim is interested in prosecution and whether the offender or a relative was injured in the accident.

60. *See* Jescheck, *supra* note 2, at 513.

61. *See* text at note 46 *supra*. A formal complaint cannot be filed in cases subject to private prosecution.

62. Under German criminal law, ordinary negligence is a sufficient basis for criminal responsibility.

63. Penal Code § 232. *See also* Jescheck, *supra* note 2, at 513–14. The special interest clause was added to the Penal Code in 1940, primarily because increasing road traffic had led to the conclusion that prosecution of traffic accidents involving bodily injuries should not depend on a discretionary determination by the victims.

64. K. LACKNER & H. MAASSEN, STRAFGESETZBUCH § 232, annot. No. 4 (7th ed. 1972); H. MÜLLER & W. SAX, KOMMENTAR ZUR STRAFPROZESSORDNUNG § 376, annot. No. 1 (6th ed. 1966); Oehler, *Die amtliche Verfolgung der leichten vorsätzlichen und fahrlässigen Körperverletzung*, 1956 JURISTENZEITUNG 630.

65. Uniform Rules of Criminal Procedure 259, 272.

Prosecuting attorneys maintain that they consistently try to comply with the Rules. In fact, they generally find special public interest, and exceptions are made only in trivial cases. For example, public charges have been brought when industrial safety laws were neglected, when a meat processing firm sold tainted products, and when the victim in a traffic accident was hospitalized or unfit to work. Cases involving only minor bruises or sprains were not deemed important enough to bring a public charge.[66]

The offender who is charged with causing bodily harm cannot appeal the prosecutor's decision that there is a special public interest requiring an investigation. Further, the prosecutor's exercise of this discretionary power is not reviewable by the courts.[67] In these cases, the departmental complaint procedure is the only available remedy.

Petty Infractions and Prosecutorial Discretion

German law distinguishes criminal offenses from petty infractions not involving the high degree of moral guilt considered necessary to justify a penal sanction.[68] Petty infractions are comparable to violations considered *mala prohibita* in American law, such as violations of traffic laws, trade and business regulations, and laws protecting the health and safety of citizens. Unlike *mala prohibita* offenses, however, petty infractions require intent or negligence for conviction.[69] The sanctions provided for petty infractions are regulatory fines instead of the harsher penalties of the Penal Code.[70] The prosecution of petty infractions and imposition of sanctions are the province of

66. See examples in text following note 58 *supra*. See also K. Homann, *supra* note 58, at 87–91.

67. 16 BGHSt 225 (1962); K. LACKNER & H. MAASEN, *supra* note 64, § 232, annot. No. 4. *But see* A. SCHÖNKE & H. SCHRÖDER, *supra* note 13, § 232, annot. No. 3.

68. See E. GÖHLER, GESETZ ÜBER ORDNUNGSWIDRIGKEITEN 10–12 (1970); H. JE-SCHECK, *supra* note 30, at 40.

69. As in criminal offenses, ordinary negligence is a sufficient basis for responsibility. *See* note 62 *supra*.

70. Petty Infractions Code [ORDNUNGSWIDRIGKEITENGESETZ] § 13 sets the maximum regulatory fine at 1,000 German marks (presently equivalent to about $400), but allows for higher sums whenever authorized by another statute. Thus fines may be as high as 100,000 German marks. *See* E. GÖHLER, *supra* note 68, at 901–44.

administrative authorities; the judiciary is not involved. Investigation and prosecution of the offenses are governed by considerations of expediency rather than the rule of compulsory prosecution, and broad discretion is given the authorities.[71] For example, in cases involving traffic violations—by far the most frequent petty infraction—the police decide whether to institute proceedings and whether pending proceedings should be terminated. The only limit on discretion is the prohibition against arbitrariness and abuse of power.[72]

The prosecuting attorney becomes involved in such cases only if a defendant files a complaint against an administrative order imposing a regulatory fine. The complaint must be filed with the authority that issued the order, but it is forwarded to a prosecutor, who takes it into court for a judicial decision.[73] While the case is not yet before the court, the prosecutor, like the administrative agency, is authorized not to prosecute. Before closing a case, however, he should check with the original authority to be sure that his decision is consistent with the policies followed by the administrative agency.[74] Contacting the authority is not required either if the decision depends solely on a question of law that the prosecutor can decide without an administrative expert, or if the prosecuting attorney is sufficiently familiar with the questions of fact involved.[75]

In fact, prosecutors rarely discontinue prosecutions of petty infractions. Most of the filtering of cases is done at an earlier stage by the administrative authorities. Prosecutors generally agree that, after a complaint is filed, a judge should make the final decision.[76] Prosecutors are ready to consider termination of the proceedings only when the order issued by the administrative agency obviously resulted from an error of law or when new evidence is introduced by the complainant.

71. Petty Infractions Code § 47.
72. E. GÖHLER, *supra* note 68, § 47, annot. No. 2.
73. Petty Infractions Code §§ 67–69.
74. Uniform Rules of Criminal Procedure 328, 338.
75. *Id.* For instance, prosecutors in the traffic section of the prosecution office usually do not need the advice of a police officer to decide a traffic case.
76. The judge, instead of deciding the issue of guilt, can close the case with the prosecutor's consent. Petty Infractions Code § 47(2).

Petty Misdemeanors and Prosecutorial Discretion

The German Penal Code places criminal offenses into three categories: felonies (punishable by imprisonment for at least one year); misdemeanors (punishable by imprisonment or fine); and petty misdemeanors (punishable by imprisonment up to six weeks or a fine not exceeding five hundred marks).[77] The category of petty misdemeanors is steadily shrinking, as many of them are reclassified into petty infractions.[78] This reclassification has been prompted by the belief that the administrative procedure used for petty infractions[79] best satisfies modern needs for speedy and flexible enforcement of the type of laws formerly in the petty misdemeanor category. The new General Part of the German Penal Code, effective on January 1, 1975, abolishes the petty misdemeanor category.

Prior to 1924, the Code of Criminal Procedure required the prosecuting authorities to investigate even the most trivial offenses, but in fact almost everyone admitted that the police took action only in important cases.[80] The economic depression of the early 1920s in Germany created pressures to simplify and speed the criminal processes,[81] and a provision was added to the Code of Criminal Procedure giving the prosecutor and police authorities discretionary power not to prosecute a petty misdemeanor where the guilt of the offender is minor and the public interest does not require a judicial decision.[82] The Uniform Rules of Criminal Procedure state that the public interest requires prosecution of a petty misdemeanor if it is committed with exceptional frequency or if the accused has previously been convicted of similar offenses.[83]

77. Penal Code § 1.
78. In 1969, for example, traffic violations were removed from the petty misdemeanor class and are now treated as petty infractions. The most common remaining petty misdemeanors are petty pilfering, causing noise or gross mischief, and acts of public obscenity.
79. *See* text and notes at notes 68–72 *supra.*
80. A. GRAF ZU DOHNA, DAS STRAFPROZESSRECHT 68 (3d ed. 1929); B. Drews & G. WACKE, ALLGEMEINES POLIZEIRECHT 158 (7th ed. 1961).
81. *See* Wolff, *supra* note 2, at 1078. *See also* J. KRÜMPELMANN, DIE BAGATELL-DELIKTE 203–4 (1966).
82. Code of Criminal Procedure § 153(1). *See* Jescheck, *supra* note 2, at 513–14.
83. Uniform Rule of Criminal Procedure 83(1). *See also id.* 82.

In practice, most petty misdemeanors are never considered by the prosecutor, because the police do not begin investigations. The prosecutor deals only with cases that the police consider important enough to be prosecuted. These cases have been carefully screened by the police,[84] so there is usually no reason for the prosecutor to fail to prosecute.

One situation in which public charges are typically brought for a petty misdemeanor is the theft of small quantities of food from supermarkets.[85] The prevalence of this type of offense has led the police and prosecutors to consider punishment a necessary means of deterrence. Exceptions have been made in a few circumstances, however, such as an indigent person taking a loaf of bread or an elderly woman who presented a doctor's report stating that she had emotional problems. Prosecutions are also sometimes brought for causing noise or gross mischief. For example, a group of juveniles were prosecuted for holding meetings in a public place with the engines of their motorbikes running, and some students were prosecuted for tampering with street signs and tipping over garbage cans.[86]

The prosecutor does not encounter many situations where the discretionary power granted to enable him to deal with petty misdemeanors is appropriate. In practice, the job of exercising discretion in these cases is performed by the police.

Prosecutorial Discretion in Misdemeanor Cases

Prosecution of misdemeanor cases may be terminated by the prosecutor with the court's consent, if the guilt of the offender is minor and prosecution is not required by the public interest.[87]

84. One court has held that the police must present all petty misdemeanors reported by a citizen to the prosecutor. Decision by the Highest State Court of Appeals of Bavaria, 1966 JURISTENZEITUNG 149. *See also* 1 LÖWE-ROSENBERG, DIE STRAFPROZESSORDNUNG UND DAS GERICHTSVERFASSUNGSGESETZ: GROSSKOMMENTAR § 153, annot. No. 11 (22d ed. 1971); H. MÜLLER & W. SAX, *supra* note 64, § 153, annot. No. 1. There is good evidence that this holding is frequently ignored. See the numerous examples presented in J. FEEST & E. BLANKENBURG, DIE DEFINITIONSMACHT DER POLIZEI 58–113 (1972).

85. For a discussion of the theft of larger quantities of food or other goods, see text at note 102 *infra*.

86. Kohlhaas, *Unzulässige Durchbrechung des Legalitätsprinzips*, 1956 GOLTDAMMER'S ARCHIV FÜR STRAFRECHT 241, 247 (listing the reckless making of noise in the vicinity of hospitals and schools as cases that should be prosecuted).

87. Code of Criminal Procedure § 153(2); *see* Jescheck, *supra* note 2, at 514.

The German category of misdemeanors is broad and includes many crimes that would be considered felonies under American law, such as larceny, embezzlement, fraud, extortion, receiving stolen goods, forgery, negligent homicide, abortion, inflicting bodily harm with a weapon, false imprisonment, dangerous driving, bigamy, and incest. This wide range of offenses in which the prosecutor can exercise discretion, subject to court approval, might give the impression that his discretion is not very limited. It must be remembered, however, that prosecutors regard compulsory prosecution and restraint of discretion as overriding principles. They generally agree that they should be reluctant to exercise their discretionary power, and they abort proceedings only in really trivial cases.[88]

Unlike the prosecutor, police authorities in misdemeanor cases are given no discretion by the Code of Criminal Procedure.[89] Police officers must investigate all reports of misdemeanors. To what extent they comply with this requirement is a difficult question. A recent study revealed astonishing instances involving the exercise of discretion by the police in misdemeanor cases.[90] Indeed, a leading authority on criminal procedure has argued that the police should not be required to investigate insignificant matters.[91]

Prosecutors must often decide whether guilt is minor and public interest nonexistent before they have fully investigated a case. Some commentators contend that any decision to close a case should be made only after gathering all of the available evidence.[92] In fact, prosecutors tend to close a case if there is a

88. K. PETERS, *supra* note 5, at 508; Dahs, *Der Anwalt im Strafprozess*, 9 AN-WALTSBLATT 171, 182 (1959). Blankenburg, *supra* note 39, at 182, indicates that in 1971 in Bade-Württemberg less than 4 percent of all cases were dropped because the offense was insignificant and prosecution was not required by the public interest. Generally prosecution offices follow the same trend, but Blankenburg, *id.* at 183, notes that there is some variance. One office, for example, discontinued about 2 percent of the cases, while another did so in 15 percent. Differences in record keeping account for some of the variances.

89. Section 153(2) of the Code refers only to the "prosecution," that is, the prosecutor.

90. J. FEEST & E. BLANKENBURG, *supra* note 84, at 58–113.

91. H. MÜLLER & W. SAX, *supra* note 64, § 153, annot. No. 3.

92. J. KRÜMPELMANN, *supra* note 81, at 208; 1 LÖWE-ROSENBERG, *supra* note 84, § 153, annot. No. 8; H. MÜLLER & W. SAX, *supra* note 64, § 153, annot. No. 2(d); Kohlhaas, *supra* note 86, at 242.

strong probability that further investigations would reveal only minor guilt.[93] A different approach would frustrate the purpose of the provision that authorized the termination of prosecution —to bring relief to overburdened prosecutors and enable them to concentrate on more serious cases.[94]

A further complication is the difficulty in determining whether a particular offender's guilt may be called minor, and public interest may be deemed nonexistent. The Uniform Rules of Criminal Procedure do not provide much guidance for these decisions in misdemeanor cases. To determine whether the offender's guilt may be deemed minor, the Rules advise the prosecutor to compare the case with similar cases involving the "average" amount of guilt.[95] The Rules also suggest that, before dropping a misdemeanor case, prosecutors consult with the administrative authorities that either reported the offense or are otherwise interested.[96]

The prosecutors usually do not make a great effort toward precisely following vague terms like "public interest" and "minor guilt." Instead, they try to develop patterns of interpretation and to ensure that similar types of offenses are treated in the same manner. Some examples will show how this process operates; at the same time, they will demonstrate the workings of the principle of restrained discretion in German criminal procedure.

Driving a motor vehicle without a license, a misdemeanor in Germany,[97] is ordinarily deemed too dangerous to the public to justify a failure to prosecute. But when, for example, a farmer's teenage son operated a tractor without a license on public roads to reach a nearby field, prosecutors were inclined not to prosecute and the courts almost always consented. They under-

93. Compare the similar problem in connection with the prosecutor's decision as to the sufficiency of the evidence. *See* text in the paragraph following note 41 *supra*. *See also* H. Müller & W. Sax, *supra* note 64, § 153, annot. No. 2(d); T. Kleinknecht, *supra* note 57, § 153, annot. No. 2(A).

94. J. Krümpelmann, *supra* note 81, at 203–4; Wolff, *supra* note 2, at 1078.

95. Uniform Rule of Criminal Procedure 83(3). *See also* J. Krümpelmann, *supra* note 81, at 208; 1 Löwe-Rosenberg, *supra* note 84, § 153, annot. No. 3.

96. Uniform Rule of Criminal Procedure 83(2). This is intended to alert them to one aspect of possible public interest. In addition, the Rules give the simpleminded advice that all of the facts of the case should be considered. *Id.* 83(3).

97. Road Traffic Act [Strassenverkehrsgesetz] § 21.

stood that farmers with small farms may be unable to pay farm-hands and must allow their sons to drive; therefore, the guilt in these cases was deemed minor and there is no significant public interest. The prosecutor's decision might be different, however, if tractor driving by young children became sufficiently widespread.

A case prosecutors often face is that of a father who is unwilling to pay for the support of his family or an illegitimate child.[98] The public interest requires prosecution of such a breach of duty, at least to protect the community from financial burdens. If the investigation reveals, however, that the defendant has begun to pay and intends to continue payments in the future, the prosecutor, with consent of the court, often closes the case. The family's or child's interest in regular support is given preference over the public interest in punishment.

In some cases a prosecutor has declined to prosecute negligent homicide.[99] A fatal traffic accident, for instance, might be primarily caused by the victim, and the defendant's guilt might be minimal. A charge of negligent homicide was brought, however, in the following case. A public playground that was opened near railroad tracks was enclosed by bushes instead of a fence. A mother neglected to pay attention to her young child in the playground; the child crawled through the bushes, went on the railroad tracks, and was killed by a train. Action was taken against the city official in charge of planning playgrounds. The prosecutor decided to prosecute, because he deemed the public interest important enough that a judge should decide the question of guilt.[100]

German prosecutors agree that abortion is a misdemeanor that should always be prosecuted. Until 1969 abortion, except when performed by the pregnant woman, was a felony and thus had to be prosecuted without exception. The present prosecutorial attitude is perhaps influenced by the previous classification. In deciding whether to prosecute an abortion offense,

98. Penal Code § 170(2). *See also* K. Homann, *supra* note 58, at 95.
99. J. KRÜMPELMANN, *supra* note 81, at 210.
100. At trial the official was found guilty of negligent homicide and ordered to pay a fine; but the conviction is on appeal. For additional cases involving negligent homicide, see text following note 148 *infra*.

prosecutors refuse to consider the vigorous movement for lib-
eralized abortion laws, statements by Members of Parliament
advocating liberalization of the law, or that women with sufficient money travel to England, the Netherlands, or Switzerland
to have abortions. Prosecutors state that the rule of compulsory
prosecution demands enforcement of the abortion laws until
they are repealed.

Despite this general rule, there have been two important instances of prosecutorial inactivity. In the troubled times soon
after World War II numerous girls were raped, and some doctors terminated resulting pregnancies in spite of the fact that
abortions are permitted only to save the mother's life or health.
Investigations were launched against some of these doctors, but,
in this special postwar situation, the top prosecutorial authorities
agreed that no charges should be brought if the abortion was
performed by a licensed physician to terminate a pregnancy resulting from rape.[101] The other example occurred a few years
ago, during the public debate on reforming the abortion laws.
About 370 women, some of them well known in German society, publicly announced in a leading magazine that they had
in the past had an abortion. Prosecutors were arguably obliged
to act; they maintained, however, that the announcements did
not constitute sufficient evidence to begin prosecution. The
police apparently did not investigate further. Thus far, none
of the women seems to have been prosecuted.

Shoplifting is usually treated in the same manner as petty
pilfering.[102] Deterrence and equal enforcement of the law are
seen as requiring prosecution of all reported offenses. National
chains of department stores usually report every offender; local
stores, however, frequently favor private settlements.[103] As a
result, the rule of compulsory prosecution arguably leads to
some inequity in enforcement of the law. Nevertheless, the rule
is strictly followed.

Strict enforcement of the pure food and water laws, particu-

---

101. von Nottbeck, *Die Straffunktionen des Staates und der Gesellschaft,* in
PROBLEME DER STRAFRECHTSREFORM 48, 60–61 (1963).

102. *See* text at note 85 *supra.*

103. The stores might ask the offender to contribute to the firm's health insurance fund or to help pay for its security system.

larly more recently, has been considered necessary. But when an elderly woman cleaned her stove and illegally discharged a small amount of oil into the public sewage system, no charges were brought. The main reason for the failure to prosecute was that, in the same city, a chemical plant was discharging toxic waste waters into the same system. The plant could not be prosecuted, since it had been arguing with the water authorities for years and had been able to delay the final order of the water authority—a prerequisite to prosecution.

When violations of the old Narcotic Drugs Act became a serious problem in Germany, violators were prosecuted, almost without exception, as a means of deterrence. Today prosecution tactics have changed. The Narcotic Drugs Act of 1972 allows the judge to refrain from imposing punishment if the defendant possessed only a small amount of narcotics for his personal use.[104] The Code of Criminal Procedure authorizes the prosecutor, with the court's consent, not to prosecute for the same reasons.[105] These provisions are often utilized. In addition, when small amounts of drugs are given to a third person, or when the offender is willing to undergo treatment, prosecuting attorneys are inclined not to prosecute.[106] In response to the growing drug problem in Germany, a proposed reform of the Code of Criminal Procedure would grant further prosecutorial discretion in drug cases. The proposal would allow prosecutors not to prosecute a small dealer if he helped police to uncover a more dangerous large dealer.[107]

A prosecutor is occasionally tempted to consider the disastrous consequences a conviction will have on the life of the accused. The defendant might hold a business position he will lose, he may be a public official who will be exposed to disciplinary measures more serious than criminal punishment, or he may be required to forfeit a trade license or concession. Considerations of this nature should not affect the actions of the

104. Narcotic Drugs Act [BETÄUBUNGSMITTELGESETZ] § 11(5).

105. Code of Criminal Procedure § 153a.

106. Juveniles are often involved in these cases. Prosecutorial discretion in cases involving juveniles is discussed at notes 164–70 *infra.*

107. ENTWURF EINES ERSTEN GESETZES ZUR REFORM DES STRAFVERFAHRENSRECHTS of May 2, 1973, Deutscher Bundestag, 7. WAHLPERIODE, DRUCKSACHE VII/551, § 153f.

prosecuting attorney.[108] The extent to which prosecutors do take the possible consequences of conviction into account cannot be determined, but these considerations probably affect some cases.[109] The concepts of minor guilt and nonexistent public interest are sufficiently flexible to cover most of these considerations,[110] but the principles of compulsory prosecution and restrained discretion are the prevalent ones. Experienced defense attorneys maintain that prosecutors sometimes are more reluctant to close a case if a prominent citizen is involved or if they are afraid that the decision will be publicly criticized.

Judicial consent to drop a prosecution is routinely given.

To drop a case the prosecutor must get the consent of the judge who would try it if a charge were brought.[111] This requirement is intended to subject the prosecutor to judicial control and thus to guarantee that the rule of compulsory prosecution will not be undermined by a single attorney. The judge, however, routinely consents.[112] Refusal to permit the case to be dropped occurs only in the rare cases in which the judge is aware of facts unknown to the prosecutor. Although prosecution offices are located only in cities, the courts are distributed all over the country. For crimes committed in rural areas, the judge in the local court might therefore be better informed about the case. In other cases, the judge might be able to inform the prosecutor that the case is part of a bigger criminal enterprise deserving punishment for deterrent reasons.

Bureaucratic restraint remains most effective.

In general, however, the requirement of judicial consent is only an indirect restraint on the prosecutor's discretionary powers. As noted above,[113] the major restraint on the individual prosecuting attorney's discretion exists within the local prosecution office. A prosecutor's decision not to prosecute because of minor guilt and nonexistent public interest must be approved by a superior in the same way as a decision to close a case for lack of sufficient evidence. In addition, the victim, if he

108. Kohlhaas, *supra* note 86, at 241.

109. *See id.* at 241.

110. *See* Heinitz, *supra* note 8, at 335; K. Homann, *supra* note 58, at 106.

111. Code of Criminal Procedure § 153(2). After the charge is brought, the judge may terminate proceedings with the prosecutor's consent. *Id.* § 153(3).

112. If consent is withheld the prosecutor may raise a formal complaint—an action that is never taken.

113. *See* text in the paragraph following note 49 *supra*.

reported the offense, is notified.[114] The victim can then object to the prosecutor's decision through a departmental complaint; the same procedure is available to the accused when the prosecutor insists on prosecuting.[115]

Conditional Termination of Proceeding for Misdemeanors and Petty Misdemeanors

Attorneys and prosecutors have pointed out that a defendant who can afford the assistance of counsel has a somewhat better chance of having his case closed. In a few cases involving misdemeanors or petty misdemeanors the defense lawyer stated to me that he had contacted the prosecutor and tried to dissuade him from bringing charges. Lawyers argue, for example, that the crime was not likely to be repeated, that the accused was injured by the offense, or that he has made full restitution to the victim. They may also indicate that the accused is willing to repent by paying a sum of money to a charitable institution. If the defense counsel is known by the prosecutor, his arguments will usually be considered. Occasionally a defense counsel might even attempt to exert some pressure on the prosecutor by stating that, if charges are brought, he will request that several additional witnesses be summoned for the trial.[116] Such tactical maneuvers are, however, rarely used. Defense counsel must be careful not to damage the good relations he enjoys with the prosecutor.

Under the Uniform Rules of Criminal Procedure the prosecutor may consider the offender's conduct subsequent to the offense and ask whether the offender's guilt can in retrospect be deemed insignificant.[117] While the defendant may not be exposed to any pressure,[118] the prosecutor is authorized to inform the accused that acts such as payment of damages to the victim might affect the assessment of his guilt. On the other hand, the Uniform Rules explicitly forbid conditioning the closing of a case on the accused paying the expenses of prosecu-

114. Uniform Rule of Criminal Procedure 79(3).
115. *See* text at note 49 *supra.*
116. H. DAHS, *supra* note 39, at 156.
117. Uniform Rule of Criminal Procedure 83(3).
118. *Id.*

tion, or contributing to the public treasury or a charitable trust.[119] During the Nazi period, prosecuting attorneys could close cases on these conditions, but after World War II they lost the right to do so.[120]

Nevertheless, prosecutions for misdemeanors and petty misdemeanors are occasionally discontinued after the accused has made a stipulated payment to a charitable institution.[121] Prosecutors do not expressly impose conditions and generally do not take the initiative. Defense attorneys, however, are aware of the possibility of working out a settlement; they usually take the first step by suggesting that their client would be willing to make a charitable donation if he could expect his case to be closed. In some instances, prosecutors felt free to suggest a higher sum if the offered contribution was too small. In a few cases, careful bargaining dragged on for weeks.

It is difficult to get reliable information about this practice, because settlement proceedings are informal and neither the prosecutor nor the accused wants any publicity. Settlements seem to be more frequent in larger cities than in other parts of the country. There are some prosecuting attorneys, however, who never engage in such bargaining. In a South German city, for example, settlements were almost entirely done away with when one of the top officials in the local prosecution office decided to reject them.

Defendants' donations to charitable institutions are usually a few hundred marks. To avoid prosecution, an automobile driver who was accused of speeding at 80 miles per hour in a 50 mile per hour zone paid one hundred marks to a church.[122]

119. *Id.* 82(4).

120. J. KRÜMPELMANN, *supra* note 81, at 205; Bartsch, *Einstellung gegen Busszahlung-Unzulässiger Freikauf von der Strafsanktion,* 1969 ZEITSCHRIFT FÜR RECHTSPOLITIK 128, 129; General Instruction given by the Attorney General of Celle to the prosecuting attorneys of his district on May 2, 1946, 1946 HANNOVERSCHE RECHTSPFLEGE 57.

121. H. DAHS, *supra* note 39, at 156; J. KRÜMPELMANN, *supra* note 81, at 226; Bartsch, *supra* note 120, at 128–29; Becker, *Bussgelder in Strafrecht,* 1972 MONATSSCHRIFT FÜR DEUTSCHES RECHT 575, 576; H. Lange-Fuchs, letter to the editor, 1969 ZEITSCHRIFT FÜR RECHTSPOLITIK 216; Schmidhäuser, *Freikaufverfahren mit Strafcharakter im Strafprozess?,* 1973 JURISTENZEITUNG 529, 532.

122. *See* decision of the District Court of Stuttgart, 1969 MONATSSCHRIFT FÜR DEUTSCHES RECHT 598. Most of the cases closed after the accused has made a charitable donation apparently involve traffic offenses.

When a public officer was prosecuted for seriously insulting a private individual, he offered to give five hundred marks to an institution that cares for crippled children.[123] A cab driver accused of an illegal citizen's arrest donated five hundred marks to the Red Cross.[124] A wholesale food dealer who had violated provisions of the food law paid three hundred marks to get his case closed. A real estate agent prosecuted for irregular business activities paid one hundred marks. One defense attorney even signed a contract of suretyship regarding his client's proposed payment.[125]

Prosecutors ordinarily agree to a settlement only in trivial cases in which there is no doubt the offender's guilt is minor. There have been a few misdemeanor cases, however, in which investigations were dropped after a voluntary donation by the accused even though serious offenses, mostly white-collar crimes, were involved. In one case, a bankrupt accused of large-scale frauds and violations of corporation laws had his prosecution averted after paying a considerable sum to the German section of the Red Cross.[126] In another, a wholesale meat dealer was charged with evading taxes and customs duties totaling 1.4 million marks; a Hamburg prosecutor ended the proceedings after the accused donated 400,000 marks to various charitable institutions.[127] This incident became a public scandal after it was revealed that 100,000 marks were paid to an association of which the prosecutor was president. The prosecutor, and the judge who had given the required consent even though he had no jurisdiction, were collecting sizable honorariums from the association for public speeches. Both were suspended from office,

123. Public prosecution in this case was said to be required by the public interest. *See* text at notes 52–57 *supra*.

124. This example, and the two that follow, are cited by Bartsch, *supra* note 120, at 128–29.

125. Decision of the District Court of Cologne, 1962 NEUE JURISTISCHE WOCHENSCHRIFT 1024. In this case proceedings were discontinued not by the prosecutor, but by the judge with the prosecutor's consent.

126. *See* K. Tiedemann, letter to the editor of *Frankfurter Allgemeine Zeitung* [a leading German newspaper], May 7, 1969, at 10.

127. *See* Schmidhäuser, *supra* note 121, at 529; DER SPIEGEL [a leading German political magazine], May 23, 1972, at 67; *Frankfurter Allgemeine Zeitung*, Jan. 12, 1972, at 3. The prosecutor was the head of the section dealing with white-collar crimes and did not need anyone's approval for the settlement.

and the prosecutor later committed suicide. A commission of inquiry set up by the Hamburg Parliament discovered that closing serious cases in return for large charitable contributions had been practiced in the city of Hamburg for some time.[128] The practice was, of course, condemned.

A case that received even more public attention was the termination of proceedings against the manufacturer of thalidomide, a sleeping pill that caused thousands of embryonic deformations and hundreds of nervous disorders.[129] The proceedings were discontinued by the court, rather than the prosecutor, after a trial of over two and a half years.[130] The court held that the guilt of the defendants, managers and chemical engineers for the firm, was minor after being exposed to a long, highly publicized trial and after the firm had offered to pay 114,000,000 marks into public trusts for the victims.[131] The public interest in a judicial resolution of the case was considered subordinate to the victims' interests in a financial settlement.[132] This case, for a number of reasons, must be called exceptional. But it indicates that the standards of minor guilt and public interest are susceptible to flexible interpretation. The practice of restrained discretion is obviously derived not from the language of the Code of Criminal Procedure, but from a consensus of the prosecutors who act according to the rule of compulsory prosecution.

A considerable number of commentators maintain that settling cases as a result of a voluntary donation by the defendant is illegal.[133] They argue that a payment cannot be deemed vol-

---

128. Schmidhäuser, *supra* note 121, at 529.

129. Decision of the District Court of Aachen, 1971 JURISTENZEITUNG 507; Bruns, *Ungeklärte verfahrensrechtliche Fragen des Contergan-Prozesses*, in FESTSCHRIFT FÜR REINHART MAURACH 469 (1972); Dahs, *Ein Monstrum verschwindet im Nichts, Die Zeit* [a German weekly paper], Jan. 1, 1971, at 36.

130. A court may close a case on the same conditions as a prosecutor.

131. Decision of the District Court of Aachen, 1971 JURISTENZEITUNG 507, at 519–20. *See also Stellungnahme der Staatsanwaltschaft im Contergan-Prozess* [reasons given by the prosecutor for his consent to close the case], 1971 DEUTSCHE RICHTERZEITUNG 45, 48–49.

132. *Id.*

133. J. KRÜMPELMANN, *supra* note 81, at 228; E. SCHMIDT, LEHRKOMMENTAR ZUR STRAFPROZESSORDNUNG, NACHTRAGSBAND I § 153, annot. No. 9 (1966); Bartsch, *supra* note 120, at 128–30; Dencker, *Die Bagatelldelikte im Entwurf eines EGStGB*, 1973 JURISTENZEITUNG 144, 149; Hanack, *Das Legalitätsprinzip und die*

untary when the defendant's alternative is prosecution.[134] The
practice has also been criticized for allowing wealthy offenders
(in particular, white-collar criminals) to buy their way out of
criminal proceedings.[135] It is further argued that pecuniary obligations should be imposed only by the trial judge, who assesses
the defendant's guilt in a public trial after hearing the evidence.[136] Nevertheless, settlement proceedings are neither expressly forbidden nor expressly allowed by the Code of Criminal Procedure and the Uniform Rules, and they are sanctioned
by some courts and a number of legal writers.[137]

Recent efforts to increase the speed of the criminal process
and to cope with the rapidly growing caseload of the prosecutors have resulted in a proposed reform of the Code of Criminal Procedure that would expand the scope of prosecutorial
discretion.[138] The proposal authorizes the prosecutor in misdemeanor cases to decide not to prosecute on the condition
that the accused makes restitution, contributes a sum of money
to the public treasury or a charitable trust, guarantees support
for a dependent of the victim, or performs some other act in

Strafrechtsreform, in FESTSCHRIFT FÜR WILHELM GALLAS 339, 344 (1973); Kern,
Wer trägt die Kostern bei Einstellung des Strafverfahrens wegen Geringfügigkeit
(gemäss § 153 Abs. 3 StPO)?, 1953 DEUTSCHE RICHTERZEITUNG 169; Schmidhäuser,
supra note 121, at 532; Trapp, *Kann die Einstellung nach § 153 Abs. 1 StPO von
der Zahlung einer Geldbusse abhängig gemacht werden?,* 1958 NEUE JURISTISCHE
WOCHENSCHRIFT 292.

134. Bartsch, *supra* note 120, at 130; Dencker, *supra* note 133, at 149;
Schmidhäuser, *supra* note 121, at 534.

135. Decision of the District Court of Cologne, 1962 NEUE JURISTISCHE WOCHEN-
SCHRIFT 1024; Bartsch, *supra* note 120, at 130; Cordier, *Kann die Zahlung einer
Geldbusse zur Voraussetzung einer Einstellung nach § 153 Abs. 1 StPO gemacht
werden?,* 1957 NEUE JURISTISCHE WOCHENSCHRIFT 1789, 1791; General Instruction
by the Attorney General of Celle, *supra* note 120.

136. J. KRÜMPELMANN, *supra* note 81, at 228; Cordier, *supra* note 135, at 1790;
Jescheck, *supra* note 2, at 514; Trapp, *supra* note 133, at 293.

137. Decision of the District Court of Stuttgart, 1969 MONATSSCHRIFT FÜR
DEUTSCHES RECHT 598; decision of the District Court of Cologne, 1962 NEUE
JURISTISCHE WOCHENSCHRIFT 1024; H. DAHS, *supra* note 39, at 156–57; T. KLEIN-
KNECHT, *supra* note 57, § 153, annot. No. 2(A); 1 LÖWE-ROSENBERG, *supra* note 84,
§ 153, annot. No. 17; H. MÜLLER & W. SAX, *supra* note 64, § 153, annot. No. 2(c);
K. PETERS, *supra* note 5, at 149; Becker, *supra* note 121, at 576; Cordier, *supra*
note 135, at 1791.

138. ENTWURF EINES EINFÜHRUNGSGESETZES ZUM STRAFGESETZBUCH OF MAY 11,
1973, Deutscher Bundestag, F. Wahlperiode, Drucksache VII, 550, Art. 19, § 153a
StPO.—After this paper was finished, the bill was passed by the German legislature (Einführungsgesetz zum Strafgesetzbuch of March 2, 1974, BGB1 I, 469).
The new law became effective on January 1, 1975.

the public interest.[139] If the accused complies with the condition within a period set by the prosecutor, the case is finally closed; otherwise, the prosecution is reopened.

This proposal has been severely criticized by commentators who argue that it would introduce uncertainty into the German criminal process.[140] It is further argued that the sanctioned bargaining procedure would result in class injustice, favoring the white-collar criminal who has sufficient means to pay.[141] Finally, the procedure may be inconsistent with the presumption of innocence, since the accused would be pressured to cooperate.[142] Despite these criticisms, the reform is likely to be approved by the legislature.

Prosecutorial Discretion and the Judge's Power to Refrain from Imposing Punishment

Under the Code of Criminal Procedure, the prosecutor may decide not to prosecute if he believes that the trial judge would be authorized to refrain from imposing a penalty even though the defendant is guilty.[143] Several provisions of the Penal Code and other statutes give the judge this power.[144] By far the most important of these applies to cases in which the consequences of the offense to the offender were of such a serious nature that a penalty is clearly pointless.[145] This provision is limited to

139. The prosecutor would need the consent of both the judge and the accused.

140. Dencker, *supra* note 133, at 149; Hanack, *supra* note 133, at 347; Schmidhäuser, *supra* note 121, at 533–36.

141. Hanack, *supra* note 133, at 349–50, 358, 363; Schmidhäuser, *supra* note 121, at 535.

142. Dencker, *supra* note 133, at 149–50; Schmidhäuser, *supra* note 121, at 534–35.

143. Code of Criminal Procedure § 153a; *see* Jescheck, *supra* note 2, at 514. The Uniform Rules of Criminal Procedure give no specific guidance for these cases. *See* Rule 84.

144. One provision, dealing with possession of a small amount of drugs for the offender's personal use, was discussed at note 104 *supra*. In addition, the judge may refrain from imposing a penalty for false unsworn testimony by a person less than sixteen years old. His discretionary power also applies if the offender committed perjury to avoid subjecting himself or a member of his family to punishment. Penal Code § 157; Code of Criminal Procedure § 60. *See also* Penal Code § 129.

145. Penal Code § 16.

cases that would not result in imprisonment of more than one year; prison sentences in Germany are, however, considerably less severe than in the United States, and even cases involving felonies may be covered.[146]

The provision was added to the Penal Code in 1969.[147] Judges are still somewhat reluctant to use it, and they have not yet reached a consensus on the cases to which it should apply. The same is true with respect to the exercise of the prosecutor's discretionary power not to prosecute such cases. As far as could be ascertained, prosecutions for felonies have never been terminated by prosecutors under this provision. For other offenses, the standard of self-inflicted harm has been liberally construed by courts and prosecutors. It includes bodily injuries and financial loss; damaging consequences to a relative of the offender or a person close to him can also be considered.[148] The reason for not imposing punishment in these cases is not the triviality of the offense, but the notion that cases of this kind do not deserve punishment.

This motivation is clear from the following misdemeanor cases in which prosecutors declined to bring charges. A mother dropped her baby boy, but did not take him to a doctor. When the baby died a few days later, it was discovered that he had a fractured skull; the injury would probably not have been fatal if it had been treated in a hospital. The mother was not prosecuted. Motorists who negligently caused accidents that resulted in serious injuries to themselves and others were sometimes not prosecuted. The same principle applied to a driver who did not harm himself, but caused injuries to a close friend and was

146. Although imprisonment of one year is the mandatory minimum for felonies, shorter sentences can be imposed if mitigating circumstances are found. For example, a provision on mitigating circumstances is included in the provisions for perjury, infanticide, robbery, and extortionary robbery.

147. Before the provision was enacted, judges tried to accomplish the same end in some cases by imposing nominal sentences. Prosecutors sometimes closed a case arguing that the accused had suffered by his own offense and thus his guilt was minor and punishment was not required by the public interest.

148. Decision of the High State Court of Appeals of Celle, 1971 NEUE JURISTISCHE WOCHENSCHRIFT 575; decision of the High State Court of Appeals of Frankfurt, 1971 NEUE JURISTISCHE WOCHENSCHRIFT 767; H. JESCHECK, *supra* note 30, at 637; A. SCHÖNKE & H. SCHRÖDER, *supra* note 13, § 16, annot. Nos. 3, 4.

deeply shocked by what he had done. The prosecutor's decision may be different, however, if the offender has acted recklessly or has previously caused other accidents.

Even reckless conduct resulting in serious harm does not always force the prosecutor to prosecute. When a farmer's wife carelessly left a box of matches on the kitchen table and her children got it and set the farm on fire, everyone in the prosecutor's office agreed that she had been sufficiently punished.[149] The same result was reached when the owner of a store lost his shop and all of his inventory in a fire caused by his failure to turn off an electric heater.

Some prosecuting attorneys are willing to attach importance also to psychic and emotional consequences the offender suffered from his crime. The majority, however, feel bound by the rule of compulsory prosecution and the idea of restrained discretion, and are willing to consider only serious physical consequences to the offender.

Prosecutorial Discretion and Multiple Offenses

If several crimes have been committed by the same person, the prosecutor is not always required to prosecute each offense. In this regard it must be noted that in Germany, the entire criminal transaction is presented to the court, rather than merely those elements selected by the prosecutor. For example, if employees of a bank were taken as hostages and a police officer killed in the course of a bank robbery, the prosecutor presents all of the facts to the court and files a charge for all possible offenses; he cannot choose to prosecute only one of the offenses and thereby bring a reduced charge.[150] A final judgment of

---

149. Negligently causing a fire is a misdemeanor in German criminal law.

150. Hence it would be useless for a defense attorney to try to bargain for such a reduction of the charge. The prosecutor in a case of this nature has no legal power to comply with the request to reduce a charge. Contrary to a statement by Professor Davis, K. DAVIS, *supra* note 1, at 195, this question is not one of prosecutorial discretion, because the prosecutor is legally prohibited from so doing. If a prosecutor illegally brought a reduced charge, it would not help the defendant; at trial, the evidence is presented by the judge, not by the prosecutor and defense counsel. The judge's actions are governed by section 155 of the Code of Criminal Procedure, which expressly provides that the judge is not bound by the legal counts of the prosecutor's charge. For details of the judge's activities at the German trial, see FOREIGN OFFICE, supra note 2, at 148–51;

conviction or acquittal is res judicata as to the entire transaction described in the charge.

The concept of the criminal transaction is not limited to acts committed in one place at one time. A transaction may include several separable acts that can be considered one episode. A series of frauds committed in several cities by a travelling salesman, the writing of numerous bad checks, or the filing of several false tax returns have all been treated as one transaction. The causing of thousands of embryonic deformations and hundreds of nervous disorders by the manufacturer of thalidomide was also held to be one criminal transaction consisting of numerous separate acts.[151]

In cases of this kind, a strict rule requiring careful investigation of each act would be an unreasonable burden on the prosecutor. He is therefore given discretion to prosecute only the most serious of the offenses, or to select typical samples out of a series of acts if the selected instances provide a sufficient basis for imposing adequate punishment.[152]

The Uniform Rules of Criminal Procedure encourage the prosecutor to exercise this discretionary power, particularly in voluminous or complex cases, to simplify and speed criminal proceedings.[153] Prosecuting attorneys usually follow this advice without hesitation. The idea of restrained discretion is not taken as seriously here as in other cases. A leading commentator has suggested that charges may be dropped even if their prosecution would be likely to increase the punishment by one-fourth.[154]

This discretion is often exercised, for example, in cases involving white-collar crimes. Investigation of these crimes is usually extraordinarily difficult because many carefully concealed transactions must be uncovered, numerous victims and witnesses must be gathered, and voluminous files and papers must be searched. In big cases the defense attorney might con-

---

Jescheck, *Germany*, in J. COUTTS, THE ACCUSED—A COMPARATIVE STUDY, 246 (1966); Schmidt, *supra* note 2, at 13–17; Wolff, *Criminal Justice in Germany* (pt. 2), 43 MICH. L. REV. 155, 162–68 (1944).

151. Bruns, *supra* note 129, at 473.
152. Code of Criminal Procedure §§ 154, 154a.
153. Uniform Rule of Criminal Procedure 86.
154. T. KLEINKNECHT, *supra* note 57, § 154a, annot. No. 2.

tact the prosecutor to dissuade him from prosecuting some of
the offenses. Careful bargaining between the defense counsel
and prosecutor might follow.

Defense lawyers have told me that, in a few cases involving
resisting arrest in addition to other offenses, prosecuting attorneys appeared to be quite willing not to prosecute that offense.
The defendant claimed that the arresting officer used more force
than necessary to make the arrest. The prosecutor was uncer-
tain whether it would be harmful to the police officer to have
the details of the arrest discussed in open court. He excluded the
offense from the charge because he felt obligated to protect the
police officer from adverse publicity.

Prosecutorial Discretion Regarding Political Crimes and Crimes Committed outside Germany

Under continental European legal doctrine, German courts
have jurisdiction over offenses committed by German citizens
outside its territory.[155] Offenses committed by foreigners are
also within German jurisdiction if directed against the German
state or one of its citizens, or if they involve, for example, illegal
distribution of narcotics, trafficking in women and children, or
counterfeiting.[156] For various reasons, prosecution of these
crimes might not be required by the public interest, even where
a serious felony is involved. The offense may already have been
punished in a foreign country, prosecution in Germany might
cause undue hardship to the offender, or prosecution of a political crime might seriously jeopardize foreign relations.

The prosecutor has broad discretionary power over offenses
committed outside Germany and political crimes.[157] His actions
are generally governed by considerations of expediency rather
than the rule of compulsory prosecution. To decline to prosecute an offense committed outside Germany, the prosecutor
must report the case to the attorney general of the state and
leave the decision to him.[158] The attorney general is in close

155. Penal Code § 3.
156. *Id.* § 4.
157. Code of Criminal Procedure §§ 153b, 153c; Uniform Rules of Criminal Procedure 84b–84f.
158. Uniform Rule of Criminal Procedure 84b.

restrained discretion is given effect in this area by the Uniform Rules of Criminal Procedure, which provide that nonprosecution of the victim is appropriate only if his offense appears less serious than the extortion in the case.[174] The language of the Code of Criminal Procedure provides no basis for such a severe limitation on this form of prosecutorial discretion.

The Code of Criminal Procedure also protects the prosecutor from being forced to decide questions of private or public law that should be left to a court or an administrative agency.[175] For example, if the mother of an illegitimate child charges the alleged father with a breach of the duty to support,[176] the prosecutor may require her to apply for a judicial declaration that the man is actually the father. The same principle applies when two fishermen have a dispute about fishing rights and one reports the other for poaching; the prosecutor may order that the fishing rights be determined by the competent administrative agency. If the question is not decided within a period fixed by the prosecutor, he may drop the case. Proceedings may be terminated in this manner only if the offense involved is not a felony; prosecution of felonies is considered too important to depend on the initiative of a private person to have a collateral question decided. The provision allowing the prosecutor to require a prior adjudication of collateral rights was added to the Code in the 1930s to relieve the prosecutor's caseload, but it is almost never used.

A further instance of prosecutorial discretion, more important than the cases discussed thus far, is not dealt with in the Code of Criminal Procedure. If the accused is too ill to stand trial,[177] or if relevant legislation or a pertinent appellate court decision is expected in the near future, the prosecuting attorney may provisionally close the case after the evidence necessary for trial has been collected. For instance, when the laws against adultery and homosexuality among consenting adults were repealed in 1969, no prosecutions for the offenses were brought in

174. Uniform Rule of Criminal Procedure 87(1).
175. Code of Criminal Procedure § 154d.
176. *See* text and note at note 98 *supra.*
177. If the accused cannot stand trial because of insanity, the prosecutor moves for a protective order issued by the judge and committing the accused to an institution. The accused need not be present at this proceeding. *See* Code of Criminal Procedure §§ 429a–429d.

the last months prior to the change in the law. There is a substantial controversy about whether the prosecutor in these cases should simply fail to prosecute or should make a formal decision to close a case.[178] The formal procedure for closing a case suggested by the Uniform Rules of Criminal Procedure [179] provides unambiguous proof of the prosecutor's decision.[180] The person who reported the offense should be informed of the prosecutor's action. On the other hand, an officially announced decision would not be necessary when the postponement is expected to be short.

Finally, the prosecutor exercises some discretion in summary proceedings. In cases involving misdemeanors and petty misdemeanors the prosecutor may, instead of taking a case to trial, apply to the judge for a penal order.[181] The application must give the details of the case and request a specific punishment.[182] The judge then decides whether to issue a penal order solely on the basis of the prosecutor's application and the file of the case. The defendant has the right to refuse the penal order and demand a trial. In this procedure the judge may not impose any punishment other than a fine or imprisonment not exceeding three months or revocation of a driver's license for not more than a year.[183] Further, he is not authorized to impose any penalty other than that requested by the prosecutor. If the judge is unwilling to act favorably on the prosecutor's application, he must set the case for trial.

The penal order is a fast and inexpensive procedure, so it is used in many cases, usually those that are easy to decide and, according to the prosecutor and the judge, do not require a public trial.[184] The penal order is, to some extent, comparable

178. 1 LÖWE-ROSENBERG, *supra* note 84, § 205, annot. No. 1; Krause, *Die vorläufige Einstellung von Strafsachen praeter legem,* 1969 GOLTDAMMER'S ARCHIV FÜR STRAFRECHT 97, 98.

179. Uniform Rule of Criminal Procedure 88.

180. Krause, *supra* note 178, at 99.

181. FOREIGN OFFICE, *supra* note 2, at 144; Jescheck, *supra* note 2, at 515–16; Langbein, *supra* note 3, at 455–58; Wolff, *supra* note 150, at 173–74.

182. Code of Criminal Procedure § 408.

183. *Id.* § 407.

184. Jescheck, *supra* note 2, at 516, indicates that more than 70 percent of the cases not closed by the prosecutor are disposed of by penal order. In 1969 the courts of the state of Hesse issued penal orders in almost 50 percent of the cases.

to the guilty plea or a plea of nolo contendere in American procedure; it can be regarded as an offer by the judge to the defendant to accept the prosecutor's charge and admit his guilt.[185] If the accused accepts the offer, the penal order is binding, like a final judgment;[186] if he objects, the summary proceedings are abandoned, and the case is tried according to ordinary procedures.[187]

By applying for a penal order the prosecutor obviously expresses interest in avoiding a full trial. This inclination is, in a few cases, taken by defense counsel as an invitation to negotiations regarding the punishment. Counsel with a client ready to admit guilt might approach the prosecutor and indicate that a penal order would be accepted if punishment did not exceed a certain limit. In these negotiations the parties obviously do not try to reach a final agreement; instead, they limit themselves to intimating their general intentions and preferences. Experienced criminal lawyers believe that prosecutors are, to some extent, willing to cooperate, but it is impossible to determine how much an offer to accept a penal order affects the prosecutor in fixing a specific penalty.

In most cases, unlike American plea bargaining, there are no negotiations regarding the offenses included in the penal order. Elimination of some charges is usually prohibited by the single-transaction rule.[188] If the defendant is accused of committing several separable criminal acts, defense counsel might suggest to the prosecutor that a penal order would be accepted if some of the offenses were excluded.

CONCLUSION

In various places this article has noted the difficulties in properly structuring prosecutorial discretion and balancing discre-

2 LÖWE-ROSENBERG, DIE STRAFPROZESSORDNUNG UND DAS GERICHTSVERFASSUNGSGESETZ: GROSSKOMMENTAR § 407, annot. No. 12 (22d ed. 1973). According to Blankenburg, *supra* note 39, at 182, penal orders were issued in about 75 percent of the cases in Bade-Württemberg in 1971.

185. See Jescheck, *supra* note 2, at 515–16; Langbein, *supra* note 3, at 456–58.
186. Code of Criminal Procedure § 410.
187. *Id.* § 411.
188. *See* text and note at note 150 *supra*.

tion against the rule of compulsory prosecution. The Code of Criminal Procedure and the Uniform Rules of Criminal Procedure try to guide discretion with fairly broad terms, but at most they provide only general guidelines. Indeed, a commentator has urged enactment of more precise legal rules and thereby stricter limits on prosecutorial discretion.[189] The wisdom of this suggestion is questionable. Because of the diversity of the problems involved, only the most detailed provisions could effectively channel the prosecutor's exercise of discretion. Such detailed provisions would probably combine with the concept of restrained discretion to reduce prosecutorial discretion to a nullity.

The present system of placing the power to control discretion within the local prosecution office seems to be far more efficient. When a prosecuting attorney decides not to prosecute, he must obtain approval of his superior and officially close the case. A file is opened for each case and recorded in a central register in the local office. Superiors are thus able to follow the activities of individual prosecutors in each case.

When a prosecutor closes a case, he gives written reasons for his action.[190] In the more difficult cases he communicates the reasons for the decision orally to his superiors. These reasons, whether oral or written, provide an effective means for supervisors to standardize and structure the exercise of discretion. At the same time, the requirement of providing reasons restricts the prosecutor's decision to close a case. If, for example, a case involves a theft from a department store, prosecution is required for deterrence and equal enforcement of the law; a proper reason for closing the case will be difficult to find. In less common cases, however, it may be easier to find an acceptable reason not to prosecute.

To complete the picture of the German prosecutor's activi-

---

189. G. KAISER, STRATEGIEN UND PROZESSE STRAFRECHTLICHER SOZIALKONTROLLE 86 (1972).

190. K. DAVIS, *supra* note 1, at 194, emphasizes that a written statement of reasons must always be given. Ordinarily prosecutors simply state that cases are closed because of insufficient evidence, minor guilt, or for some other equally uninformative reason. Blankenburg, *supra* note 39, at 189.

ties, one more factor should be mentioned. The prosecutor in a sense is isolated from the facts. He must investigate all offenses brought to his attention, but the initial investigation is typically performed by the police authorities. The police are legally obligated to investigate all cases other than petty misdemeanors and petty infractions, but in fact this duty is not discharged. Police officers exercise broad and unknown discretionary powers. As long as no file is opened and no superior is present, the police officer's discretion cannot be controlled. A study of police activities found that the police often did not investigate cases in which a misdemeanor or even a felony was committed.[191] Police officers freely exercise their power to label acts as criminal or not criminal, and they often downgrade traffic violations. Thus, most cases are screened and sifted before they reach the prosecutor.

Despite the rule of compulsory prosecution for prosecutors and a complementary requirement for police officers, some offenses are almost never prosecuted in Germany. Wildcat strikes, for example, are classified as misdemeanors under the Penal Code, yet no prosecution has followed various highly publicized wildcat strikes. There is illicit work in Germany on a large scale, but the statute against illicit work is never enforced. Running a brothel is a misdemeanor under German criminal law, but brothels thrive in numerous cities. Police officers and prosecutors are certainly aware of their existence, but proceedings are initiated only in extraordinary cases.[192]

The German system of criminal procedure, unlike the American system, tries to control prosecutorial activities with the rule of compulsory prosecution and the concept of restrained discretion. There are, however, some examples of discretionary power that are not expressly authorized by the Code of Criminal Procedure. It can be argued that the development of these exceptions indicates that the German system works effectively only because of this unofficial police and prosecutorial discretion.

[margin handwritten note: Exceptions permit the compulsory prosecution rule to work.]

191. J. FEEST & E. BLANKENBURG, *supra* note 84, at 58–113.
192. Heinitz, *supra* note 8, at 335.

American Comments on American and German Prosecutors

Americans can probably learn more from Professor Joachim Herrmann's piece on the German prosecutor's discretion than from any other part of this symposium. His article surpasses in comprehensiveness all other descriptions of that system that have been published in English.[1] It therefore is especially valuable. An American reader, I think, wants the details of the way the German system operates, a summary of that system in large perspective, and a comparison and contrast with the American system. Since Professor Herrmann provides only the first, I must attempt to provide the other two. What I shall say about the German system will be mostly dependent on his factual reporting, but the analysis will be wholly mine and will differ a bit from his view. The summary and the contrast tend to run together, and I shall not try to keep them separate.

The central question is whether or to what extent the German prosecutor has discretionary power to withhold prosecution when the evidence and the law justify prosecution. A hasty reader of the Herrmann article may note that nine-tenths of the discussion is about discretion and may get the impression that discretion is very considerable. Yet the opposite impression could grow out of Professor Herrmann's conclusory statement that "the idea of compulsory prosecution . . . is today considered the fundamental principle governing the prosecutor's activities." [2] The whole truth, I think, lies somewhere between the two opposite impressions. Here, in a single sentence, is what I believe to be an accurate characterization of the German system: The principle governing prosecution for felonies is compulsory prosecution, but the main element in the prosecution of minor crimes or misdemeanors is controlled discretion, not compulsory prosecution.[3]

1. The Herrmann article cites the other literature in note 2. In addition, Langbein, *Controlling Prosecutorial Discretion in Germany,* 41 U. Chi. L. Rev. 439 (1974), has unusual historical depth and unusual breadth of understanding.
2. Page 17.
3. In my earlier treatment of the subject, my key sentence was: "Whenever

By far the most important statutory provision affecting the prosecutor's discretionary power with respect to misdemeanors or minor crimes is § 153 of the Code of Criminal Procedure. The translation by Dr. Horst Niebler, published in 1965, uses the term "minor crime" for what Professor Herrmann translates as "misdemeanor." It provides: "If in the case of a minor crime the guilt of the actor is insignificant and if the public interest does not require enforcement, the prosecution may terminate the proceedings, with the consent of the court. . . ." This provision probably affects more than 90 percent of minor crimes when the evidence is sufficient to justify prosecution.[4] Through such words as "insignificant," "the public interest," and "may" it definitely confers discretionary power on the prosecutor, and therefore the system with respect to minor crimes is not one of compulsory prosecution. But the exercise of discretion is subject to "the consent of the court"; it is also subject to other important controls, to be described below, and that is why I think it is one of controlled discretion.

"Controlled discretion."

The three concepts I find necessary to compare the German and American systems of prosecutors' powers are compulsory prosecution, uncontrolled discretion, and controlled discretion. The German system is a mixture of the first and third, and the American system is almost entirely the second. The startling fact is that the German prosecutor's discretion is consistently controlled all along the line, and that the American prosecutor's discretion is consistently uncontrolled all along the line. The exceptions to what has just been said about the German system probably affect less than 10 percent of prosecuting ac-

the evidence that the defendant has committed a serious crime is reasonably clear and the law is not in doubt, the German prosecutor, unlike the American prosecutor, is without discretionary power to withhold prosecution." DISCRETIONARY JUSTICE: A PRELIMINARY INQUIRY 194 (1969). That remains a sound statement. But I would now change a footnote statement that "With respect to certain small misdemeanors, including traffic offenses, both the police and prosecutors in Germany have a substantial power of selective enforcement" by deleting the word "small."

4. For a discussion of misdemeanor cases not included in the 90 percent, see the Herrmann article. The term "minor crime" does not include noncriminal infractions, discussed in his "Petty Infractions and Prosecutorial Discretion." And as of the beginning of 1975, it excludes petty misdemeanors, discussed in "Petty Misdemeanors and Prosecutorial Discretion."

tivity with respect to felonies and minor crimes. The exceptions concerning the American system may be in the neighborhood of only about 1 percent.[5]

COMPULSORY PROSECUTION

Compulsory prosecution means that a prosecutor has no discretionary power to withhold prosecution when he finds that the evidence and the law justify prosecution. In the German system it is regarded as a part of the principle of legality. The Code of Criminal Procedure provides in § 152: "I. To prefer the public charge is the function of the prosecution. II. Except as otherwise provided by law, it is obliged to take action in case of all acts which are punishable by a court and capable of prosecution, so far as there is a sufficient factual basis." German prosecutors interpret the word "obliged" literally. If the "except" clause were omitted, the system would be one of compulsory prosecution. About nine-tenths of felonies are subject to compulsory prosecution; the main ones that are not are political crimes, juvenile crimes, crimes committed outside Germany, crimes for which the defendant has been extradited, unusual felonies for which the court has power to impose no penalty, a lesser crime in a series of crimes when the defendant is prosecuted for a more serious crime in the series, and a defendant too ill to stand trial. The bulk of misdemeanors are taken out of compulsory prosecution by § 153, quoted and discussed above.

The American system has in it a slight touch of compulsory prosecution in non-criminal areas. For instance, the statutes

5. The exceptions are very rare and have to do mainly with occasional cases in which courts review prosecutors' discretion. Examples are People v. Walker, 14 N.Y.2d 901, 252 N.Y.S.2d 96, 200 N.E.2d 779 (1964); United States v. Steele, 461 F.2d 1148 (9th Cir. 1972); Littleton v. Berbling, 468 F.2d 389 (7th Cir. 1972), reversed on other grounds in O'Shea v. Littleton, 414 U.S. 488 (1974). Judicial review of prosecutors' discretion in noncriminal cases is more common; examples are Dunlop v. Bachowski, 95 S.Ct. 1851 (1975); Adams v. Richardson, 480 F.2d 1159 (D.C. Cir. 1973); Terminal Freight Handling Co. v. Solien, 444 F.2d 699 (8th Cir. 1971), cert. denied 405 U.S. 996 (1972); Medical Committee for Human Rights v. SEC, 432 F.2d 659 (D.C. Cir. 1970), dismissed as moot 401 U.S. 973 (1971); Universal-Rundle Corp. v. FTC, 352 F.2d 831 (7th Cir. 1965), reversed on other grounds 387 U.S. 244 (1967).

impose a mandatory duty on the transportation agencies (Interstate Commerce Commission, Civil Aeronautics Board, and Federal Maritime Commission) to prosecute for violations,[6] and Title VI of the Civil Rights Act of 1964 requires the Department of Health, Education and Welfare to institute proceedings to withhold federal funds for violations.[7]

THE BACKGROUND OF AMERICAN UNCONTROLLED DISCRETION

Uncontrolled discretion is not merely the dominant element in the American system of prosecuting; it is almost the exclusive element. Compulsory prosecution is virtually nonexistent, and the prosecutor's discretion is almost completely immune to legal control. Although statutes commonly provide for compulsory prosecution, the prosecutors themselves have established a system that is at variance with the statutes, and their system prevails—mostly because the courts do not review it, but partly because, in the rare cases in which the courts do review it, the courts weakly acquiesce. The best example is the statute conferring power to prosecute for federal crimes, 28 U.S.C. § 547: "Except as otherwise provided by law, each United States attorney, within his district, shall—(1) prosecute for all offenses against the United States. . . ." From the words "shall" and "all" one might suppose that prosecution is compulsory. But prosecutors have interpreted those words to mean "may" and "some," and their interpretation has prevailed. The system is not based on legislative intent; it is based on unplanned drift over nearly two centuries. The statute was first enacted as a part of the Judiciary Act of 1789: "And there shall be appointed in each district a meet person learned in the law to act as attorney for the United States . . . whose duty it shall be to prosecute in such district all delinquents for crimes and offences, cognizable under the authority of the United States." [8]

6. An example is the Federal Aviation Act, providing that "it shall be the duty of the . . . Board to investigate the matters complained of," 49 U.S.C. § 1482. On that ground a court set aside a Board dismissal of a complaint in Trailways of New England, Inc. v. CAB, 412 F.2d 926, 931–32 (1st Cir. 1969).

7. The provision was unanimously enforced by an eight-judge court in Adams v. Richardson, 480 F.2d 1159 (D.C. Cir. 1973). See note 14 *infra*.

8. 1 Stat. 92.

"Duty" and "all" seem clear, and apparently no legislative history about the provision exists. The statute has never been amended, except by codification. Interpretation has to be limited to the statutory words. A later provision in the same section says that each U.S. attorney shall prosecute proceedings for the collection of fines, penalties, and forfeitures "unless satisfied on investigation that justice does not require the proceedings," and no such clause applies to the words "shall . . . prosecute for all offenses."

The courts have nevertheless allowed prosecutors to create such an "unless" clause that Congress has not enacted. In a codification "duty" was replaced by "shall," which is interpreted to mean "may," the equivalent of "no duty." In 1868 in a case involving a forfeiture, the Supreme Court generalized about the power of district attorneys in all cases: "Public prosecutions . . . are within the exclusive direction of the district attorney. . . ."[9] In an outstanding case, when a district judge thought a U.S. attorney was abusing his discretion by dismissing an indictment, he nevertheless held that he could not review, quoting from the Confiscation Cases that the court "cannot control" the prosecutor, and adding that "he is not even required to give a reason for dismissal."[10] Even when the complaining party, the grand jury, and the judge insisted on prosecution, the U.S. attorney was held to have unreviewable power to refuse to issue indictments required by the grand jury.[11] When a U.S. attorney allowed A to plead guilty to a misdemeanor but convicted B of felony, even though A and B allegedly committed the crime together, Judge Burger (now Chief Justice) wrote an opinion refusing to inquire whether equal justice had been denied. The well-supported theme of the opinion was that "the existence of very broad discretion in the prosecutor has long been taken for granted."[12] That statement reflects the universal understanding that now prevails.

Whether or not the legislative intent in the 1789 statute and

9. Confiscation Cases, 7 Wall. (74 U.S.) 454, 457 (1868).

10. United States v. Woody, 2 F.2d 262 (D. Mont. 1924).

11. United States v. Cox, 342 F.2d 167 (5th Cir.), cert. denied 381 U.S. 935 (1965).

12. Newman v. United States, 382 F.2d 479, 480 (D.C. Cir. 1967).

in its later codified versions was that the words "duty," "shall," and "all" should be given their literal meaning, the system clearly is not one of compulsory prosecution.

THE DOZEN FACETS OF UNCONTROLLED DISCRETION

Nor does the American system of prosecuting provide for controlled discretion. In the following twelve ways, the American system is one of uncontrolled discretion. (1) Discretionary decisions to prosecute or not are unguided by statutory standards. The American system is flagrantly illogical: when legislative bodies delegate discretionary power, hundreds of cases have held that constitutional principles require guiding standards; but when such officers as police and prosecutors assume undelegated discretionary power, the courts have never required guiding standards. (2) Courts do not require prosecutors to provide guiding standards through exercise of a rulemaking power, and prosecutors almost never volunteer such rulemaking.[13] (3) When a prosecutor learns of a crime, he need not investigate. When

[handwritten margin note: Prosecutor discretion might not meet delegation requirements.]

13. All administrators, including prosecutors, have power to issue interpretative rules explaining how they exercise their discretionary power. When Congress created the Wage-Hour Administration in 1938, it debated the question whether to confer a rulemaking power upon the Administration and decided not to. The Wage-Hour Administration nevertheless systematically stated its enforcement policies in periodic Interpretative Bulletins, now published in the Code of Federal Regulations. When a problem of applying the statute came to the Supreme Court, it followed the Interpretative Bulletin, declaring that the administrator's interpretations, "while not controlling upon the courts by reason of their authority, do constitute a body of experience and informed judgment to which courts and litigants may properly resort for guidance." Skidmore v. Swift & Co., 323 U.S. 134, 140 (1944).

A typewritten document entitled "The Prosecutor's Discretion—A Statement of Policy of the Office of District Attorney of Harris County," dated April, 1974, provides "General Guidelines" for initiating prosecution. The guidelines are broad and vague, but they are a beginning, and Carol S. Vance, the district attorney of Harris County, Texas (including Houston), deserves commendation for them.

Another exceptional example is ANN. REP. U.S. ATT'Y GEN. 59–60 (1938), asserting in an antitrust context: "Not only judicial policy but prosecuting policy must be developed by precedent and on publicly stated grounds. . . . Businessmen are entitled to know what kinds of situations will lead to prosecution. . . . The Department of Justice recently announced a policy under which there would be issued a series of public statements throwing light on the prosecuting policy with respect to the antitrust laws." The system was cut off by the war a few years later, but it can be revived.

At last in late 1974 the California District Attorneys Association issued two

he investigates, he need not continue the investigation, no matter what evidence he finds. He is not required to close the file.
If he chooses, he can become too busy on other cases and never
complete the investigation or make a decision on the question
whether the evidence justifies prosecution. (4) He is not required to state his findings of fact, either to the victim or to a
superior, a court, or the public. He need not state findings in
the file. (5) When he decides questions of law or policy or discretion, he need not state reasons. Indeed, he need not *have*
reasons. (6) He need not compare cases. He need not follow
precedents. He need not be consistent. He can go north in one
case and south or east in the next case, even if the two cases
are identical. (7) He can pick and choose in enforcing statutes,
enforcing one fully, consistently refusing to enforce a second,
and enforcing a third only if and as his whim impels him. A
legislative body may labor long and diligently to establish a
statutory policy; the prosecutor may nullify it. Charges that
the civil rights legislation which Congress enacted during the
1960s has been largely nullified by lack of enforcement during
the 1970s may often be excessive, but they contain a good deal
of truth.[14] (8) No matter how clear the evidence of serious
crime, the American prosecutor may agree to accept a plea of

volumes of "Uniform Crime Charging Standards." The preface expresses the
hope that the Standards "can serve as an example to the rest of the nation. . . ."
And well they may, for they are beautifully formulated, and the organization
plans to keep them up to date. Instead of the usual pretense that prosecutors
"just enforce the law," the authors forcefully assert that "Prosecutorial discretion is an integral part of the American criminal justice system. . . ." The
Standards may prove to be the first long step toward a profound revolution in
the American system of prosecuting.

For a thorough and scholarly presentation of a thesis that "it is both feasible
and desirable to develop comprehensive and detailed policy statements governing the exercise of prosecutorial decision-making and that significant prosecution
resources should be allocated to the task of developing such policy," see
N. Abrams, *Internal Policy: Guiding the Exercise of Prosecutorial Discretion,*
19 UCLA L. REV. 1, 57 (1971).

14. In Adams v. Richardson, 480 F.2d 1159 (D.C. Cir. 1973), the eight-judge
court unanimously affirmed an order of the district court requiring HEW to
commence enforcement proceedings against 74 school districts violating Title VI
of the Civil Rights Act of 1964, to commence enforcement against 45 districts
in presumptive violation of a Supreme Court ruling, to demand of 85 other
districts an explanation of racial disproportion in apparent violation of the
Supreme Court's requirement, and to take other action. The statute "authorized
and directed" enforcement.

guilty in return for charging a lesser crime. (9) His discretion is not subject to review by any superior administrative authority if he is the top prosecutor of a governmental unit (city, county, state, or federal government). (10) Even if he acts arbitrarily and capriciously and abuses his discretion, his decisions are normally immune to judicial review. (11) He is not required to act openly. When he decides not to investigate or not to prosecute, he can usually cover up an abuse of discretion by keeping silent. In that manner he can cut off criticism by the press and the public. (12) When an American prosecutor fails to prosecute, the victim of the crime typically has no legal remedy even if he can prove that the prosecutor has abused his discretion.

THE GERMAN CONTROLLED DISCRETION

On every one of the dozen items above, the American prosecutor has uncontrolled discretion and the German prosecutor has controlled discretion. The German system is one of compulsory prosecution with respect to felonies, so the controlled discretion is ordinarily limited to misdemeanors or minor crimes. With respect to those crimes, here are the facts of the German system on each of the dozen items: (1) The statutory standards of § 153 —guilt which is insignificant, and public interest not requiring enforcement—are broad and vague, but they do have enough meaning to satisfy the usual American requirement of standards to guide delegated power. Furthermore, their interpretation in particular cases tends to become a matter of law, calling for consistency in interpretation—with the result that not only is discretion guided, but for many cases it is eliminated. (2) Through the Uniform Rules of Criminal Procedure, the German states have significantly elaborated the statutory standards. Such rulemaking to guide prosecutorial discretion contrasts with the absence of it in the United States. (3) When a German prosecutor learns of a crime, he has to open a file. Then he has a supervised duty to close the file. When he fails to investigate or when he discontinues an investigation, he has to explain his decision in the file. He cannot simply forget about the case, as an American prosecutor often does. (4) The German prosecutor must state his findings in the file. A finding may be very brief, such as "insufficient evidence." But such a brief finding must be supported by what is in the file. The evidence discovered will be set out or summarized, and the nature of the needed evidence that has not been found can be discerned. (5) The prosecutor must state reasons for each decision on questions of law or policy or discretion. (6) Although German prosecutors do not think in terms of administrative precedents, although they do not rummage in their own files to find their own precedents, and although they are allowed to change their minds, they do not have the freedom of their American counterparts to decide one way on Monday, another way on Tuesday, and a third way on Wednesday. Their supervisors require a greater degree of responsibility. But the occasions for supervisors to impose such a requirement are infrequent. (7) German prosecutors do not pick and choose in enforcing statutes. Their practice is to enforce all statutes, although occasional instances of nonenforcement can be found; the case of the prominent women who published statements that they had violated the abortion law is an example. But Professor Herrmann is unclear as to whether a prosecutor has a duty to act in absence of a report from the police or from another administrative authority,[15] and, at all events, such nonenforcement in Germany is not common practice, as it is in the United States, but is highly exceptional. (8) The German prosecutor has no discretion to trade a lesser charge for a plea of guilty. The closest approach to American plea bargaining is the system of the penal order, under which the prosecutor, the defendant, and the judge may enter into a three-way agreement that the defendant will plead guilty and will be given a specified sentence. What seems to me remarkable is not that such a three-way agreement is permissible when the sentence is more than

15. He says in "Petty Misdemeanors and Prosecutorial Discretion" that "the prosecutor deals only with cases that the police consider important enough to be prosecuted." But he implies that the prosecutors, not merely the police, neglected to prosecute the women who openly acknowledged that they had violated the abortion statute.

three months, but that such an agreement is not permissible when the sentence is less than three months. Legislation may soon become effective that will limit penal orders to cases involving no imprisonment. (9) An extremely important feature of the German system is that decisions of all prosecutors up to the Minister of Justice of the Federal Republic are subject to review by superiors. Except for the Minister, no prosecutor in Germany is free from administrative review, as are top prosecutors of American governmental units at all levels. The superiors Professor Herrmann consulted all said that they review every case; although he thinks his sampling insufficient to support a statement that superiors throughout Germany review every case, the reality seems to be that each prosecutor acts in each case as though his action in that case is likely to be reviewed. (10) In contrast with the American unreviewability of prosecutors' discretion, § 153 of the German Code of Criminal Procedure, governing more than 90 percent of decisions not to prosecute minor crimes on grounds other than insufficiency of evidence, requires the prosecutor to act "with the consent of the court." Although Professor Herrmann says that court approval is "routine," any American reader can form his own judgment as to whether its requirement is likely to have a good deal of effect on prosecutors' behavior. What would be the effect of a requirement of judicial consent on an American prosecutor who tends to postpone investigation indefinitely, who gives in to political or other pressures, or who acts capriciously in other ways? Would the mere requirement that he be prepared to explain his decision to the judge be likely to change his behavior? (11) The German Code does not require the prosecutor to act openly, but the requirement of judicial consent means that the determination becomes a part of the public records of the court, so that potential criticism by the press and the public is not cut off. But the other protections are so plentiful and effective that the occasion for such criticism rarely arises. (12) The German prosecutor's decision not to prosecute is reviewed not only by the court and by his superiors but is also subject to check by the victim of the crime, who can file a motion with the highest state court of appeals, and can also file a departmental complaint with the prosecutor's superior. If he chooses, the victim may constitute himself a last line of defense against abuse of prosecutorial discretion.

AMERICAN DRIFT

The German system seems carefully planned in each facet. The American system seems obviously unplanned. Would any sane planner create the dozen items of uncontrolled discretion? The American system is the product of an accretion over nearly two centuries of small decisions which prosecutors have made largely in their own interest.

The system of judicial unreviewability for abuse of prosecutorial discretion is likewise unplanned, although it stems from judges rather than from prosecutors. It grew up during the nineteenth century, when the dominant attitude was that "interference of the Courts" with executive departments "would be productive of nothing but mischief." [16] Even as late as 1900 the Supreme Court summarized the law: "It has been repeatedly adjudged that the courts have no general supervising power over the proceedings and action of the various administrative departments of government." [17] But during the twentieth century, judicial reviewability of administrative discretion has become the norm, because of the discovery that courts can provide a meaningful check without substituting judgment.[18] The unreviewability of prosecutors' discretion for abuse is a clear departure from the prevailing assumption that courts should protect against abuse of administrative discretion.[19] The main reason for the departure, I think, is that the present generation of judges recoils from reviewing prosecutors' discretion because the volume of new judicial business would be so enormous. The

16. Decatur v. Paulding, 39 U.S. (14 Pet.) 497, 516 (1840).
17. Keim v. United States, 177 U.S. 290, 292 (1900).
18. See 4 K. DAVIS, ADMINISTRATIVE LAW TREATISE § 28.04 (1958, and 1970 Supp.).
19. Prosecutors are administrators. Federal prosecutors are subject to the Administrative Procedure Act. The law that governs them is administrative law. It is high time that the American legal profession change its longstanding assumptions to the contrary.

judges' own interests largely determine their decisions on a major question of judicial policy. I do not speak critically; on the contrary, the very best judges take the most pride in the quality of their work, and they are the ones who properly have the strongest interest in protecting that quality against the threat of a huge volume of new business. The conflict of interest is not the fault of the judges, for it is built into the system. So the unreviewability continues, although the exceptions around the edges are growing.[20]

The lack of legal control of American prosecutors' discretion is aggravated by the unplanned failure to insulate their discretionary choices from political or other ulterior influence. We insulate our judges; one with an interest at stake may not ethically try to influence a judicial decision outside the courtroom, and by and large the ethical principle is obeyed. But we have no such tradition against influencing prosecutors' decisions. Senators and Congressmen often help constituents to escape prosecution; their intervention is called "casework" and is not generally deemed unethical. And a U.S. attorney or other

[handwritten margin note: Ex parte influence on prosecutors.]

20. To a very slight extent, American judges are beginning to realize that they can use a very gentle touch in controlling prosecutorial discretion. For instance, in DeVito v. Shultz, 300 F. Supp. 381 (D.D.C. 1969), the court ordered the Secretary of Labor to file with the court a memorandum of explanation of why a case was not prosecuted under the Labor-Management Reporting and Disclosure Act. A courageous judge who imposes that requirement on the secretary in a regulatory matter may impose the same requirement on a U.S. attorney in a criminal matter. Cases requiring regulators to explain nonprosecution decisions include Environmental Defense Fund v. Ruckelshaus, 439 F.2d 584 (D.C. Cir. 1971), and Medical Committee v. SEC, 432 F.2d 659 (D.C. Cir. 1970), dismissed as moot 401 U.S. 973 (1971). In Terminal Freight Handling Co. v. Solien, 444 F.2d 699 (8th Cir. 1971), cert. denied 405 U.S. 996 (1972), the court invented some useful conceptualism in reviewing the prosecutorial discretion of a regional director of the NLRB. It said the prosecutor could have (1) "absolute discretion," (2) mandatory duty with "some latitude" or with "limited prosecutorial discretion," or (3) unqualified mandatory duty to prosecute. It chose the second. When judges discern the potentialities of that idea, combined with a gentle touch as in DeVito, they may become less reluctant to assert judicial power to review.

In Dunlop v. Bachowski, 421 U.S. 560 (1975), the Supreme Court held the prosecutorial discretion of the Secretary of Labor under the Labor-Management Reporting and Disclosure Act to be judicially reviewable. The decision has great promise as a precedent that may open the way to judicial review of denials of prosecution in criminal cases, for the difference between criminal cases and this civil case is small enough that a court can easily disregard it if it is so inclined.

prosecutor is peculiarly vulnerable to political influence, because most American prosecutors use their offices as stepping stones to higher political positions. They often welcome requests for favors from those who wield political power, because they may ask favors in return. When the politician says to the prosecutor, "Please do me a favor; X is an old friend of mine and a good fellow," the prosecutor may initially decide to deal with the X case on its merits. But he may then postpone action, with the idea that when he gets to it he will decide it on the merits; then after a while he finds that the X case is too stale to pick up. He has done the favor without ever making a decision to do it. Or perhaps he has even done the favor after making a decision not to do it.[21]

Americans can learn from Germans how to formulate a plan to insulate prosecutors from political influence. The main idea is to make the prosecutor's office nonpolitical—to make it *not* a stepping stone to elective office. Anyone who becomes an assistant prosecutor in Germany is on a career ladder; he has reached that position on his merits, and if he goes on up the ladder, perhaps to the bench, the promotions will be on the merits. He can gain nothing by doing a politician a favor; he is more likely to lose by doing such a favor. The tradition is strongly established that each political party avoids any advantage for its own members (as against members of the opposition party) in promoting prosecutors or judges. The result is that favors are neither asked nor expected.

Some Questions about Future Planning

If a planned system were substituted for the present product of American drift, what would it look like? The answer, of course, must be based on many studies and on much give and take among minds that differ. I am not yet prepared to advance my own answer, but, stimulated by the German system, I shall suggest what I think some of the questions are.

21. Most American prosecutors are dedicated, conscientious, and incorruptible. But some are not, and all shades of deviation result from varying degrees of temptation. Surely a sound system has to be built on the observation that not all men are angels.

Would the tiny bit of compulsory prosecution we now have be vastly expanded? Would new statutes, instead of authorizing enforcement, sometimes authorize *and require* enforcement? Would statutes prescribe not only what is legal and illegal but also what is to be enforced, what is not to be enforced, and what is within prosecutors' discretionary enforcement powers? Would statutes be written so that prosecutors would have only the discretionary powers delegated to them, and not the powers that they assume in contravention of statutes? Would courts then enforce the legislative intent behind such statutes?

Would statutes confer upon prosecutors a rulemaking power and require them to exercise it as far as feasible? Would courts impose on prosecutors a requirement of rulemaking? Would prosecutors' discretion in individual cases be limited in the main to interpreting facts and interpreting law, and would their discretion to decide issues of policy be limited by the requirement that they make most of their policies through rulemaking? Would policy making in individual cases nevertheless interact with rulemaking, so that the rules would continually be in process of further development and refinement?

Would a prosecutor have an obligation to investigate, or to explain in the file why he does not? Would each significant decision have to be supported by findings and reasons? Would a prosecutor be bound either to follow his own precedents or to write a reasoned opinion explaining why he overrules them? Would all statutes be tailored to enforcement capacities so that unenforced statutes would disappear? Or, instead, would the rulemaking power be allowed to take care of obsolete statutes when legislative bodies fail to keep abreast of the times? Would silent nullification of legislative policies by unstudied nonenforcement be disapproved to such a degree that officials would be suspended or discharged for indulging in it?

Would pleas of guilty and agreed sentences still be possible, but would statutes and rules assure more emphasis on the merits of the question of how long the defendant should be imprisoned, so that decisions would no longer be based exclusively or mainly on the convenience of the prosecutor?

Would every prosecutor in the nation, except the top one in

the federal government and in each state, have a superior in a hierarchical organization, who would in fact provide an effective check upon the exercise of discretionary power by his subordinates? Would U.S. attorneys lose the independence they now enjoy, and would they become career officers in the Department of Justice, appointed by and responsible to the attorney general, and not politically appointed? Would independent city and county prosecutors be eliminated, and would each state attorney general have subordinates in each locality? Would popular election of local prosecutors thus be ended?

Would ex parte influence of a prosecutor's decision be deemed unethical, just as ex parte influence of a judge's decision is now deemed unethical? Would prosecutors reject such influence, just as judges now do?

Would victims of crimes have rights with respect to requiring or bringing prosecutions, as they always have had in England [22] and as they have to a lesser extent in Germany? Would Americans at last realize that denial of rights even to victims of continuing crimes is a major flaw in the American system?

Would principles of administrative law, such as those that now apply to federal officers in general, at last be extended to the administrative officers who are called prosecutors? Would the ignorance and inattention that gives rise to the idea that prosecutors are necessarily exempt from those principles at last give way to the discovery that officers who administer criminal justice (prosecutors and police) are administrative officers, and that their agencies are administrative agencies? Would prosecutors' discretionary determinations become reviewable for abuse of discretion, just as the discretionary determinations of nearly all other administrative officers and agencies are reviewable for abuse of discretion?

I do not know the answers to these questions, and I shall study them further. But I think I can answer the question of whether Americans have too long neglected such questions.

---

22. Private citizens have always been allowed to bring prosecutions in England, except that a few limited statutes have cut off that right. In addition, a private citizen may compel law enforcement officers to enforce criminal statutes. Regina v. Commissioner, Ex parte Blackburn [1968] 2 Q.B. 118, and [1973] 2. W.L.R. 43.

CHAPTER THREE

The Application of the Antitrust Rules of the EEC Treaty by the Commission of the European Communities

KARL MATTHIAS MEESSEN

The definition of "discretionary power" and of "confining," "structuring," and "checking" as used in this essay is derived from K. C. Davis's book, *Discretionary Justice*.[1] The term "discretionary power" is wider than its German equivalent "Ermessensfreiheit," because it also covers the choice among legal interpretations of which, in German theory, only one is correct, and even "illegal discretionary action."

This account of facts is based on the rather comprehensive record of the Commission's activities as laid down in the *Annual Report,* the *Bulletin,* and the *Official Journal of the European Communities,* and also on interviews with eight officials of the A-level (requiring a university degree) at the seat of the Commission in Brussels.

This report was written in spring, 1973, covering the time until December 31, 1972. Some references to later publications were added in January, 1974.

When we study the exercise of discretionary power by the Commission of the European Communities, we must keep in mind that the structure of the European Communities differs from the constitutional system of parliamentary democracies. The legislative function within the European Communities is exercised by organs which have little in common with their

1. K. Davis, Discretionary Justice: A Preliminary Inquiry (1971).

counterpart in municipal law; the Treaty itself corresponds to statutory law and to the constitution. The Treaty has been concluded by the governments of member states and has entered into force after it had been approved by the respective parliaments. The legal basis of community law can be altered only by a new treaty; in reality, it can hardly be altered at all. In addition to the Treaty there exists a body of secondary law passed by two nonparliamentary organs: the Council of Ministers and the Commission. The role of the European Parliament—in the treaties of Paris and Rome called the Assembly—is a rather limited one. The Parliament has to be heard during the course of passing Community legislation. The administrative functions rest with the Commission. The members of the Commission are appointed by the governments of member states. They do not derive their mandate from Parliament, which may, however, by a vote of censure force the Commission to resign. The Court of the European Communities corresponds to municipal courts in both its functions and its structure. Despite those differences, the authority of the Commission resembles that of national administrative bodies in one important aspect: in the field of antitrust law the Commission is entitled to make individual decisions which are directly binding upon any party. This common feature appears to permit a comparative study of the exercise of discretionary power.

The substantive antitrust law of the EEC Treaty is contained in two provisions:

Article 85

1. The following shall be prohibited as incompatible with the common market: all agreements between undertakings, decisions by associations of undertakings and concerted practices which may affect trade between Member States and which have as their object or effect the prevention, restriction or distortion of competition within the common market, and in particular those which:
   (a) directly or indirectly fix purchase or selling prices or any other trading conditions;
   (b) limit or control production, markets, technical development, or investment;

(c) share markets or sources of supply;

(d) apply dissimilar conditions to equivalent transactions with other trading parties, thereby placing them at a competitive disadvantage;

(e) make the conclusion of contracts subject to acceptance by the other parties of supplementary obligations which, by their nature or according to commercial usage, have no connection with the subject of such contracts.

2. Any agreements or decisions prohibited pursuant to this Article shall be automatically void.

3. The provisions of paragraph 1 may, however, be declared inapplicable in the case of:

—any agreement or category of agreements between undertakings;

—any decision or category of decisions by associations of undertakings;

—any concerted practice or category of concerted practices; which contributes to improving the production or distribution of goods or to promoting technical or economic progress, while allowing consumers a fair share of the resulting benefit, and which does not:

(a) impose on the undertakings concerned restrictions which are not indispensable to the attainment of these objectives;

(b) afford such undertakings the possibility of eliminating competition in respect of a substantial part of the products in question.

Article 86

Any abuse by one or more undertakings of a dominant position within the common market or in a substantial part of it shall be prohibited as incompatible with the common market insofar as it may affect trade between Member States. Such abuse may, in particular, consist in:

(a) directly or indirectly imposing unfair purchase or selling prices or other unfair trading conditions;

(b) limiting production, markets, or technical development to the prejudice of consumers;

(c) applying dissimilar conditions to equivalent transactions with other trading parties, thereby placing them at a competitive disadvantage;

(d) making the conclusion of contracts subject to acceptance by the other parties of supplementary obligations
which, by their nature or according to commercial usage,
have no connection with the subject of such contracts.[2]

Any reader of these two articles will admit that the scope of
possible interpretations is extremely wide. The rules of procedural law contained in the Treaty are even less complete; they
consist essentially of a single provision which authorizes the
Council to "adopt any appropriate regulations or directives to
give effect to the principles set out in Articles 85 and 86" (Article 87). The Council shall act on a proposal from the Commission and after consulting the Assembly. This authority, which
also relates to substantive law, may for specific purposes be
delegated to the Commission.

By Regulation 17/62, which became effective on March 13,
1962, the Council entrusted the Commission with the power to
make individual decisions which are directly applicable to and
binding upon any party to whom they may be addressed. The
exercise of this power will be discussed here. It may therefore
be appropriate to enumerate the different types of measures the
Commission may take under Council Regulation 17/62 and to
indicate the principal areas of discretionary power.

1. Parties may apply for a negative clearance according to
Article 2 Council Regulation 17/62. In cases in which Articles
85 and 86 are inapplicable, the Commission must grant such
negative clearance.[3] Some authors take the view that the Commission is free to grant a negative clearance if it regards a violation of Articles 85 and 86 as minor and therefore does not see
any cause for action on its part.[4] To date no decision of this
kind has been reported, and it seems doubtful whether the
Commission is really permitted to proceed in this manner, because it is generally held that third parties could by way of an
action force the Commission to require the termination of any
infringement of Articles 85 or 86.[5] By now this question has

2. English Text of EEC Treaty, Commandpaper 4864, Miscellaneous No. 5
(1972).
3. Mestmäcker, with further references.
4. Mestmäcker, *supra* note 3, at 524.
5. Ibid.

probably lost its practical importance, because minor infringements are no longer regarded as covered by Articles 85 or 86 (*de minimis* rule). The discretionary power of the Commission mainly follows from the vagueness of substantive law which includes terms such as "restriction of competition," "effects on trade between member states," "abuse of a dominant position." But it must be emphasized that the Commission's interpretation of such terms is subject to the control of the Court of the European Communities. Sometimes negative clearances have been granted only after the agreements concerned had been adjusted according to proposals by the Commission.[6] Furthermore, the Commission exercises some discretionary power by selecting certain cases for decision while other applications remain pending for more than then years.

2. Agreements, decisions, and practices which violate Article 85 § 1 but qualify for an exemption under Article 85 § 3 have to be exempted by the Commission upon notification by one of the parties concerned.[7] In addition to the interpretation of Article 85 § 1, the Commission is charged with the task of applying Article 85 § 3, which implies the evaluation of economic advantages to be expected from certain restrictive practices. The judicial control of the Commission's evaluation is limited. In the words of the Court of the European Communities: [8] "Besides, the exercise of the Commission's powers necessarily implies complex economic judgments. Judicial control of these judgments should respect that character by limiting itself to an examination of the materiality of the facts and legal descriptions which the Commission deduces therefrom." The problem of selective enforcement is a matter of great importance in exemption cases: recently the Court of the European Communities ruled that "new cartels" (i.e., cartels agreed upon after March 13, 1962) are void unless the Commission grants

6. *See,* for example, decision of June 30, 1970, in re Kodak, 1970 COMMON MARKET LAW REPORTS (RESTRICTIVE PRACTICES SUPPLEMENT) D19, hereafter CMLREP (R.P.SUPP).

7. If a case qualifies for an exemption, the Commission has no discretion concerning whether to exempt the practices or not. *See* Mestmäcker, *supra* note 3, at 516. The wording of article 85 § 3 (". . . may . . . be declared inapplicable . . .") is misleading in this respect.

8. Judgment of July 13, 1966, Grundig-Consten, 1966 CMLREP 418, 477.

an exemption under Article 85 § 3.[9] It follows that parties performing such an agreement bear the risk of an eventual refusal of the exemption, because third parties may bring actions for damages incurred in the time between the notification and the Commission's decision. Additional scope for the exercise of discretionary power is conferred upon the Commission by Article 8 § 1, which provides: "A decision in application of Article 85 (3) of the Treaty shall be issued for a specified period and conditions and obligations may be attached thereto."

3. In cases which are covered by Articles 85 § 1 or 86 and which do not qualify for an exemption under Article 85 § 3, the Commission will "by decision require the undertakings or associations of undertakings concerned to bring such infringement to an end" (Article 3 Regulation 17/62). This decision, being correlated to the denial of a negative clearance and an exemption, presupposes an identical scope of discretionary power in interpreting its legal requirements. In addition to such an order "to cease and desist," the Commission may order certain measures of relief [10] and combine its order with the imposition of default fines according to Article 16 Regulation 17/62.

4. Whenever undertakings intentionally or negligently infringe Article 85 § 1 or Article 86 of the Treaty, Article 15 Regulation 17/62 authorizes the Commission to impose fines. The amount may range from 1,000 to 1,000,000 units of account (one unit of account was equal to one U.S. dollar until the devaluation of the dollar in 1972). Fines may even exceed one million units of account up to the amount of 10 percent of the turnover in the preceding business year of each of the undertakings participating in the infringement. In fixing the amount of the fine, the Commission is bound to take account of only the "gravity" and the "duration" of the infringement.

Thus at the outset we find those elements that usually allow both the use and the abuse of discretionary power: the vagueness of substantive law, authorization of two executive bodies to implement the law, and the limited extent of parliamentary

9. Court of the European Communities, Judgment of February 6, 1973, Haecht II, 1973 CMLReP 287.
10. Mestmäcker, *supra* note 3, at 524, 525.

control of the body making individual decisions. Administrative acts in the field of antitrust law often have far-reaching consequences, both for the individual and for the general public. Any abuse of discretionary power would involve the risk of serious damage.

The next part of this paper will show how the Council, and especially the Commission, contributed to confining, structuring, and checking the exercise of discretion. Despite the generally good results achieved in this respect, some problems will need to be further examined: the extent of undiscovered restrictive practices, the problem of selective enforcement, and the choice of measures.

CONFINING DISCRETION

The substantive law of Articles 85 and 86 was defined by regulations relating to special economic sectors, such as traffic, and by regulations providing for exemptions of certain categories of restrictive practices under Article 85 § 3. The latter type, called "group exemptions" or "block exemptions," will serve as an example for the Commission's procedure of confining discretion.

Within a year after the enactment of the basic procedural regulation (Council Regulation 17/62) 37,000 cases were pending with the Commission. The Commission started handling those cases by grouping them into categories of restrictive practices. Exclusive dealing agreements and license agreements were the largest groups. After deciding a couple of cases concerning exclusive dealing agreements, the Commission prepared a draft regulation providing for group exemptions of certain categories of exclusive dealing agreements and of license agreements. The draft was adopted by the Council in 1965 as Council Regulation 19/65. This Regulation did not by itself exempt any agreements from the application of Article 85 § 1, but authorized the Commission to issue a regulation describing the type of exempted agreements in greater detail as soon as it gained further practical experience. In the field of exclusive dealing agreements, the Commission did gain some additional experience by making various individual decisions. Furthermore, it had the benefit of several rulings of the European Court concerning such agreements. In 1967 the Commission regarded itself as sufficiently experienced in this field, but not in the field of license agreements, and it adopted a regulation by which only certain categories of exclusive dealing agreements were exempted (Regulation 67/67). In the same year the Commission was able to terminate 13,041 pending cases, nearly all of which qualified for an exemption under Commission Regulation 67/67.[11] The Commission at the beginning of 1973 was preparing a new regulation providing for group exemptions, based on Council Regulation 19/65 concerning license agreements, on which various decisions have been made during 1971 and 1972. In the meantime the Commission has caused the Council to issue a regulation authorizing the Commission to exempt certain categories of specialization agreements (Council Regulation 2821/71). The Commission has already made use of this authority by Regulation 2779/72 of December 21, 1972. The same division of the same administrative body (namely, the Commission's General Directorate on Competition) is responsible for drafting Council regulations, Commission regulations, and the decisions which precede and later apply such regulations.

STRUCTURING DISCRETION

Council Regulation 17/62 not only provides the legal basis of the Commission's competence to make individual decisions, but also contains a set of rules of administrative procedure which contribute to structuring the exercise of discretionary power. Those rules are further elaborated by several Commission Regulations implementing Council Regulation 17/62. The procedural position of the enterprises concerned, of third parties, and of member states will now be described, and then the internal decision-making process inherent in the hierarchical structure of the Commission will be outlined, followed by some remarks on the Commission's information policy.

11. KOMMISSION DER EUROPÄISCHEN GEMEINSCHAFTEN, ERSTER GESAMTBERICHT ÜBER DIE TÄTIGKEIT DER GEMEINSCHAFTEN S. 60 (1967).

Before the Commission may make any decision of the categories enumerated above, it is directed to communicate the points of complaint to the enterprises concerned and to give them an opportunity to submit their views in writing. In its decisions the Commission does not deal with objections that have not been communicated to the enterprises. This procedure is compulsory in case a fine or a periodic penalty payment will be imposed. Third persons who applied for a decision requiring termination of an infringement of Articles 85 or 86 are entitled to be heard by the Commission, if the Commission intends to deny the application. If other persons showing a sufficient interest apply to be heard, the Commission offers them the opportunity to make known their views in writing within a certain time limit. Hearings are held upon request if the persons asking for them show a sufficient interest, or if the Commission proposes to impose on them a fine or a periodic penalty payment. The Commission is free to offer any other person the opportunity to express his views orally.

The position of private parties, however, does not seem to be entirely satisfactory. Even when hearings are held, the Commission is not directed to respond to any question submitted by private parties or to comment upon the views expressed by them,[12] and hearings are allowed only once in a fairly early stage of the proceedings. Private parties are not informed of—and may therefore not comment upon—the views expressed by the governments of member states, or upon additional evidence which may have been discovered after the hearing.[13] This observation leads to a further point of criticism: the Commission has always denied any right of private parties to inspect its files.[14] In fact, neither the Treaty nor the secondary law confers such a right on the parties. It may be argued that a limited right to inspect the files follows from general principles of law which are common to the legal orders of the member states and therefore constitute binding Common Market law.

The Commission is directed to proceed in close and constant

12. Graupner, *Commission Decision-Making Process on Competition Questions,* COMMON MARKET LAW REV. 291, 304 (1973).

13. Sedemund, *Das Verfahren der EWG in Wettbewerbssachen,* EUROPARECHT 306, 315 (1973).

14. *Id.* at 313.

liaison with the competent authorities of the member states. Such authorities may comment upon the proceedings at any time. The Commission has to consult a special Advisory Committee on Restrictive Practices and Monopolies (composed of officials appointed by each Member State) before it may take any final decision of the categories enumerated above. The Commission invites the Advisory Committee for a joint meeting; the invitation is accompanied by a summary of the case, together with an indication of the most important documents and a preliminary draft decision. The report of the consultative proceedings is annexed to the draft decision but is not made public,

Whereas the authorities of member states take part in the decision-making process on the basis of rather elaborate rules provided by Regulation 17/62, the contribution of the Commission's administrative units to the drafting of decisions follows from the organizational structure of the Commission.[15]

In principle, all decisions are made by the Commission itself. A simple majority of members suffices. One member of the Commission is responsible for the General Directorate on Competition, which is in charge of the antitrust proceedings. The Legal Service, also headed by a General Director, is represented in the Commission by the President of the Commission. It exercises important advisory functions in the courts of drafting decisions of legal relevance. The power to make preliminary decisions has been delegated by the resolution of the Commission to the member of the Commission in charge of competition. This power has been partly subdelegated to the head of the General Directorate on Competition. The General Directorate is a body consisting of some fifty officials with university education; it is subdivided into five directorates, most of them consisting of several divisions. The organizational structure is hierarchical. Any action against the public has to be taken by the General Director or one of the directors.

In ordinary cases the internal decision-making process may be described as follows. Applications for negative clearances, notifications in order to obtain an exemption, and requests by third parties are filed with Directorate E (Inspection). Director-

15. As to the following *cf.* Graupner, *supra* note 12, 295*ff.*

ate E starts informal investigation and tries to obtain additional information. The file is then transferred to the head of Directorate B (Individual Antitrust Cases outside the Sectors of Energy and Steel), who selects one official as rapporteur of the case and usually another official as adviser. These two officials continue investigations in close cooperation with Directorate E. In this stage of the procedure many cases are settled informally.

Only in a few cases are proceedings formally opened by a decision according to Article 9 Council Regulation 17/62. Since this decision has to be made by the entire Commission and since its only legal effect consists in terminating concurrent jurisdiction of national authorities, it is usually postponed as long as possible. The first draft of a decision to open proceedings has to be prepared by Directorate B. The draft is then forwarded to Directorate A (General Competition Policy). Within Directorate A, Divisions 2 (Legal Acts and Matters of Principle) and 3 (Economic Affairs) comment upon the draft. Further comments are provided by the Legal Service. Profound differences of opinion between Directorate B on the one hand and Directorate A or the Legal Service on the other hand are quite common; such differences usually have to be settled on a high level. Afterward the draft is revised by Directorate B, which submits it to the General Director. The General Director forwards it to the competent member of the Commission, who puts it on the agenda of the Commission. Within the Commission opposing views are often advanced by the General Directorate on Industry or the General Directorate on Agriculture, the attitude of those General Directorates being rather favorable to cartel agreements. The Commission's decision to open proceedings is communicated to the member states. Directorate B then continues investigations in close cooperation with Directorate E. It has to draft the points of complaint. This draft is subject to the same procedure as the draft of the decision to open proceedings, with one difference: the final decision is taken not by the Commission itself, but by the member of the Commission in charge of competition. Later, investigations continue. In this phase written and oral hearings of the concerned parties and of third parties are held. Then Directorate B prepares the first draft of the final decision, which is again submitted to Divisions 2 and 3 of Directorate A and to the Legal Service. After the draft has been revised, the Consultative Committee on Restrictive Practices and Monopolies enters its comments. Such comments may necessitate complete reformulation of the draft, which then has to be submitted for comments to Divisions 2 and 3 of Directorate A and to the Legal Service. The revised draft proceeds to the General Director, then to the competent member of the Commission, and finally to the Commission itself.

Before the final decision is made, three or four years have usually passed, and at least twenty officials with university education have had some influence on preparing its contents. The lack of effectiveness is obvious. Furthermore, it may be asked whether the attention of officials is more directed to resolving internal differences of opinion than to administering individual justice. Both problems might be solved by delegating the decision-making power to independent committees of three or five officials. German authors have repeatedly proposed to establish such a body on the model of the German Federal Cartel Office.[16]

The substantive antitrust law of the EEC Treaty is likely to present even more problems of interpretation than any national antitrust law. As the preceding paragraph shows, the Council and the Commission have taken various steps to reduce the scope of possible interpretations by issuing regulations implementing the substantive law of the Treaty. Besides those measures of confining discretion, the Commission has pursued a continuous policy of elucidating its own line of thought and thereby structured the exercise of its discretionary power. In doing so it has resorted to various instruments of information policy.

The Commission has issued several general statements on its interpretation of Articles 85 and 86. For instance, a statement of June 2, 1970, gives a clear idea of how the Commission applies the *de minimis* rule in the field of antitrust law. According to § 2 of this statement, the Commission regards agreements as

16. Sedemund, *supra* note 13, at 323 with further references.

not violating Article 85 if, under certain conditions, the turnover of the products affected by the agreement does not amount to more than 5 percent of the total turnover of such products within the Common Market. Though statements of this nature do not constitute legal rules,[17] they are not without legal effects. Persons relying on a statement issued by the Commission could certainly not be fined under Article 15 of Council Regulation 17/62, because any infringement would be based neither on intent nor on negligence. Furthermore, decisions of the Commission which are not in conformity with such a statement might be contested because of abuse of discretionary power.[18]

The Commission has also issued general publications which are of a less formal character. For instance, the *Memorandum on the Process of Concentration in Industry,* published in 1966, exercised considerable influence. The enforcement policy has also been laid down in many addresses delivered partly before the European Parliament, by members of the Commission, and by the head of the General Directorate on Competition. Papers published in law reviews are always accompanied by a little note to the effect that the views expressed are those of the author and not of the Commission, but it is notorious that superiors check the articles written before they are published. Thus the author's opinion is unlikely to differ much from the Commission's official attitude.

The publication of individual decisions plays a highly significant role in structuring discretion. The Commission is fully aware of this effect and, since the entry into force of Council Regulation 17/62, it has pursued a careful policy of developing its interpretation of Articles 85 and 86. In fact, as will be discussed later, the Commission has selected only those cases for decision which appeared to suit as model cases. The Commission is generally free to alter its legal interpretation; only in exceptional cases may it be held to have confined its discretion by continuous earlier practice.[19] The Commission has also used

17. Mestmäcker, *supra* note 3, at 40.
18. Nass, *Probleme des europäischen Kartellverfahrens,* EUROPARECHT 100, 122 (1970).
19. *Cf.* FUSS, DIE EUROPÄISCHEN GEMEINSCHAFTEN UND DER RECHTSSTAATSGEDANKE 45 (1968).

the method of deciding spectacular cases in order to draw the attention of business circles to the risk of noncompliance with the antitrust rules contained in the EEC Treaty. This explains the fact that all the decisions imposing fines because of infringements of substantive antitrust law have been published, although the publication of such cases is not obligatory.

On the other hand, all decisions on negative clearances, the prohibition of restrictive practices, exemptions, and various other matters must be published. Usually the entire text of the decision is published, but this is not mandatory. Of course, those parts of any decision that refer to business secrets are excluded from publication. Some cases which are settled in a preliminary stage are reported by the Commission in the *Bulletin of the European Communities,* in the *Annual Report of the Commission,* and sometimes also by way of communications to the press. Usually the facts are stated so clearly that the legal reasoning of the Commission becomes intelligible. The opening of formal proceedings and the issuance of the points of complaint are sometimes communicated in the same manner.

Finally, the Commission renders extensive legal advice by general publications such as leaflets and forms for application, etc. Very often businessmen or their lawyers contact officials of the General Directorate on Competition to obtain information on individual cases either in writing or by telephone. The general policy is to render such information in a most generous but noncommittal way.

CHECKING DISCRETION

The decision-making process itself provides for the careful deliberation of decisions issued by the Commission. In view of the hierarchical structure of the General Directorate, officials are controlled by their superiors. Even informal settlements have to be signed either by the Head of the General Directorate himself, or by a director after the Head of the General Directorate has given his consent. In the case of informal settlements, the involvement of the Legal Service is not obligatory. Thus the procedure preceding an informal decision to close the file is less complicated than the one described above. It has been maintained that, because of the burdensome procedure outlined above, officials tend to prefer shortcuts in the interest of a speedier conclusion.[20] This might diminish the opportunity for mutual checking. If an official within Directorate B decides to delay investigations in a certain case, it is doubtful whether this will always come to the attention of his superiors. Disciplinary complaints against officials are rare.

The European Parliament exercises a certain amount of control by way of inquiries concerning individual cases. Members of Parliament may by written questions take up any individual matter. The impact of such questions should not be underestimated. The Commission is forced to investigate the matter and to publish a fully reasoned answer. A high percentage of those questions seems to be based on complaints brought to the attention of the deputies by businessmen. The political control exercised by the European Parliament is less significant, as was pointed out in the introductory remarks.

The scope of judicial control within the European Communities in general and within the field of European antitrust law in particular is extremely wide. The entire conduct of the Commission—except recommendations and opinions—is subject to judicial control. The Court of Justice has unlimited jurisdiction to review decisions whereby the Commission has imposed a fine or a periodic penalty; the Court may cancel, reduce, or increase the amount. Complaints of violation of legal rules and of abuse of discretionary power may be filed by member states, by the Council, and by natural or legal persons in cases in which the decisions are addressed to them or in which they are directly and individually concerned. Complaints may also be based on inaction by the Commission. But the practical relevance of such actions should not be overestimated. Third parties who may suffer from the slow procedure of the Commission hesitate to sue the Commission under Article 175 of the ECC Treaty because they fear the reaction of the members of a cartel, which can be much quicker and more effective than any measures taken by the Commission. Therefore, ex-

20. Graupner, *supra* note 12, at 305.

perts in antitrust law are not surprised that only one action of this nature has been brought so far. The complaint was based on the ECSC Treaty and prompted action by the Commission before the Court could pass a decision.[21]

THE EXTENT OF UNDISCOVERED RESTRICTIVE PRACTICES

Articles 85 and 86 of the EEC Treaty constitute binding law since 1958. Council Regulation 17/62, which provides the instruments of enforcement, became effective on March 13, 1962. It may be appropriate to give a survey of the final decisions made until the end of 1972.

In only five cases (two in 1969, three during the last quarter of 1972) have fines been imposed for violations of Article 85. In eleven cases (four of them during the last quarter of 1972) certain practices have been prohibited by way of a decision of the Commission. Negative clearances have been granted in twenty-three cases (one in 1972). In seven of these cases the Commission expressly stated that the negative clearances could be granted only after the companies had adjusted their practices in certain respects. In twenty-two cases (three in 1972) exemptions were granted under Article 85 § 3, four of them after certain adjustments had been made. Whereas the figure of formally decided cases is rather low, mention must be made of more than 30,000 cases which were settled without formal decision.

Does this record show general compliance with the European antitrust law, or does it hint at any inefficient enforcement policy by the Commission? The extent of undiscovered practices is always hard to guess, especially in view of the Commission's failure to publish (and apparently failure to prepare)[22] a report of impact control of EEC Antitrust Law. The following factors have to be taken into account. Within liberal economies there is a general tendency towards cartelization which can be stopped only by antitrust laws. At the end of

21. Court of the European Communities, Judgment of July 8, 1970, E. Hake & Co., 1970 CMLRep o. 426.
22. Steindorff, *Zur Entwicklung des europäischen Kartellrechts*, ZEITSCHRIFT FÜR DAS GESAMTE HANDELSRECHT 203, 208 (1973).

1972 the European Communities consisted of six countries with a total population of nearly 200 million. European antitrust law is applicable whenever restrictive practices are apt to affect trade between Member States adversely; in view of the already existing customs union, many restrictive practices of a certain volume are likely to affect trade between Member States and, therefore, to enter the scope of European antitrust law. The Federal Republic of Germany is the only Member State possessing a strict national antitrust legislation; Italy has no antitrust laws. Under these circumstances it cannot be assumed that the European antitrust laws were generally complied with.

The unimpressive record of enforcement has several causes. The Commission has only a limited staff working on antitrust investigation; however, the compliance with the complicated procedure prescribed by Council Regulation 17/62 and by the Commission's internal regulations requires much time. The investigatory procedure lacks efficiency. The Commission has very much relied on notifications and applications by participants—which rarely contain information about any clear infringements of Articles 85 and 86. Waiting for complaints by third parties does not solve the problem—third parties do not always file such complaints, either because they do not have a sufficient knowledge of European antitrust law or because they fear the reaction of the participants. The annual average of some twenty cases opened ex officio in the time between 1962 and 1971 (the figures of 1972 show an increase to forty-four) appears to be rather low. Under Article 12 Council Regulation 17/62 the Commission is entitled to pursue inquiries by economic sectors. The Commission has used this right only in two instances. To some extent the Commission's performance in the field of antitrust investigation must be attributed to a deliberately cautious policy. In some Member States the merits of antitrust law are still debated in business circles and among politicians. Perhaps the Commission felt that an overzealous enforcement policy could undermine its whole concept of antitrust policy. The sharp increase in the number of adverse decisions at the end of 1972 might, however, indicate a change of policy. Whereas during the first ten years of applicability of Council Regulation 17/62 the Commission imposed fines in only two cases, it did so in three cases within the last two months of 1972. Furthermore, the Sugar case of January 2, 1973, which resulted in fines amounting to 9 million units of account, may be mentioned. Perhaps these efforts constituted the Commission's answer to the widespread criticism voiced against its enforcement policy.[23]

THE PROBLEM OF SELECTIVE ENFORCEMENT

When Council Regulation 17/62 became effective, many applications for negative clearances, notifications to obtain exemptions, and complaints of alleged violations of Articles 85 and 86 were filed with the Commission. At the end of March, 1964, the Commission found itself confronted with 37,000 such applications, notifications, and complaints. It is interesting to see how the Commission tackled the problem.

In July, 1963, the Commission adopted a resolution containing principles for the selection of cases. The full text of this resolution has apparently not been published, but its contents were reported in one of the general reports of activity.[24] The Commission gave priority to complaints filed or in which litigation is pending before courts of Member States, cases which are not notified, cases concerning Article 86, and cases in which restrictive practices are notified before they are put into operation. Furthermore, the Commission planned to select cases for decision according to the nature and importance of the restrictive practices, and according to the economic impact of these practices on the Common Market. It also planned to decide cases in different economic sectors and to take account of the facts as precedents for future interpretation of Articles 85 and 86. This resolution is not legally binding and, in practice, only the principles mentioned in the last sentence appear to have been followed. For instance, it took the Commission

23. *Cf. Frankfurter Allgemeine Zeitung*, October 21, 1972, at 17.
24. KOMMISSION DER EUROPÄISCHEN WIRTSCHAFTSGEMEINSCHAFT, 7. GESAMTBERICHT ÜBER DIE TÄTIGKEIT DER GEMEINSCHAFT 73ff. (1 April 1963–31. March 1964).

nearly five years to decide on the Cement Makers' Agreement.[25] In this case an action to perform a cartel agreement had been filed with a national court. The Court of Appeal of Brussels had stayed proceedings in order to give the Commission an opportunity to decide upon the question of granting a negative clearance. The first decisions concerning Article 86, which were also to receive top priority, were decided in 1971,[26] but the Commission complied with the plan to decide cases of different categories so as to use them as precedents.[27] It divided all the pending cases into different groups according to legal criteria such as license agreement, franchise agreement, etc. One case was selected at random from the largest group. If it appeared to be suitable as a test case, investigations were continued in order to prepare it for a decision; after deciding the test case, similar cases were terminated informally. The decision in the Rieckermann/AEG-Elotherm case[28] guided informal decisions terminating 1,073 similar cases.[29] When several test cases had been decided, the Commission enacted Regulation 67/67, which provided for a group exemption. Thousands of pending cases were terminated informally according to this regulation, and the number of pending cases was diminished considerably—from 36,401 on March 31, 1965, to 23,296 on December 31, 1969, and 2,873 on December 31, 1972. New cases did not present any major problem; they arose at the rate of about a hundred a year after 1967. The enlargement of the European Communities on January 1, 1973, caused a new wave of applications; however, the number of 37,000 will not be reached again, because Commission Regulation 67/67 exempted many contracts from the duty to register.

The way in which the Commission coped with the large number of cases cannot be regarded as unsound. It enabled the Commission to decide a maximum number of cases and at

25. Decision of May 5, 1969, 1969 CMLReP (RPSupp) D 15.
26. Decision of June 2, 1971, Re GEMA, 1971 CMLReP (RPSupp) D 35; decision of December 9, 1971, Re Continental Can Co. Inc., 1972 CMLReP (RPSupp) D 11.
27. See also above, "Confining Discretion."
28. Decision of November 6, 1968, 1968 CMLReP (RPSupp) D 78.
29. Kommission der Europäischen Gemeinschaften, 3. Gesamtbericht über die Tätigkeit der Gemeinschaften 62 (1969).

the same time to structure its interpretation of Articles 85 and
86 for the general benefit of the public. But the exclusive application of this criterion for the selection of cases disregards
the interests of private parties. If private parties, after having
given notice of an agreement in order to obtain an exemption
under Article 85 § 3, dare to perform such an agreement, they
bear the risk of an eventual refusal of the exemption.[30] A few
months' waiting would no doubt be tolerable, but the average
now is three to four years; indeed, some cases have been
pending for a decade. Under these circumstances selecting
only test cases for decision certainly helps structure discretion but may not always be in conformity with the exigencies of
individual justice.

THE CHOICE OF MEASURES

If the Commission finds that certain practices violate Article
85 or Article 86, it may choose one of the following measures:
It may prohibit such practices by a decision according to Article
3 § 1 Council Regulation 17/62 and order additional measures
as outlined above in the first section. It may, before prohibiting
such practices, address recommendations to the companies according to Article 3 § 3 Council Regulation 17/62. It may, under certain additional conditions, impose fines according to
Article 15 Council Regulation 17/62. It may make an informal
request to the companies to put an end to the infringement.
Finally, it could take no action at all, though it might then be
sued for failure to act.[31]

The Commission is subjected to influences exercised from
various sides, but it does not appear to have yielded to any
undue pressure. The Commission and its civil service have
developed a considerable sense of independence. It may, however, be asked whether the enforcement policy of the Commission really corresponds to the rather strict wording of the substantive law.

30. See the first section of this article; see also Steindorff, *supra* note 22, at 217.
31. See the end of the section on "Checking Discretion."

Companies which are prepared to follow formal or informal recommendations of the Commission and to adjust their practices run almost no risk of being fined because of infringements prior to the adjustment.

Many cases were terminated after the participants informed the Commission that they had adjusted their practices according to the requirements of certain test cases or of Commission Regulation 67/67. In some cases the adjustments apparently covered only minor points and did not render the whole agreement legal. In 1972 the Commission, according to its own statement, "started" checking whether earlier decisions have been complied with.[32]

There is no evidence that the Commission has ever decided not to take action in a case in which it had knowledge of an infringement of Articles 85 or 86. Yet the possibility exists. In view of the large number of cases pending, the decision not to take action rests mainly with the individual official: a decision to stop proceedings in a certain case comes to the attention of only a small number of officials. Furthermore, proceedings may be delayed by an official who does not promptly forward the file to his superiors or colleagues. I was not able to find out whether the discretionary power has ever been abused in this respect. Several proceedings have been terminated because the third party who had originally filed a complaint lost interest in the matter.[33] Since it is known that participants of restrictive practices exercise some pressure on outsiders who dare to file complaints, it may be asked whether the facts would really have justified any ex officio action on the part of the Commission.

Making a decision depends not only on the merits but also on such factors as the choice between a highly complicated procedure and a less formal one. This observation may serve

32. KOMMISSION DER EUROPÄISCHEN GEMEINSCHAFTEN, 6. GESAMTBERICHT ÜBER DIE TÄTIGKEIT DER GEMEINSCHAFTEN (1972).

33. KOMMISSION DER EUROPÄISCHEN WIRTSCHAFTSGEMEINSCHAFT, 10. GESAMTBERICHT ÜBER DIE TÄTIGKEIT DER GEMEINSCHAFT 94, 96 (1. April 1966–31. March 1967); KOMMISSION DER EUROPÄISCHEN GEMEINSCHAFTEN, 1. GESAMTBERICHT ÜBER DIE TÄTIGKEIT DER GEMEINSCHAFTEN 61 (1967).

as an additional explanation of the fact that comparatively few cases were decided in accordance with the very complex procedure as outlined earlier.

American Comments on Antitrust Enforcement

Discretion in antitrust administration is broad both in the European Communities and in the United States. In order to make a comparison, I shall divide discretion in such activity into two parts—discretion in adjudication of cases that have already been instituted, and discretion with respect to initiating a proceeding.

Discretion of the first kind seems to be about equal in Europe and America, as it rests on legal terms of about the same degree of vagueness. The key words in the European substantive law are "restriction of competition," "effects on trade between member states," and "abuse of a dominant position." The key words of federal antitrust law in the United States are "restraint of trade" and "monopolize." Both in Europe and in America, administrators and courts give meaning to the vague words in the process of adjudicating cases; precedents in earlier cases guide the determinations in later cases, so that bodies of case law confine and guide discretion. Administrators try to be consistent in granting clearances. In Europe the discretion exercised by administrators in fixing penalties is subject to full judicial review, and in the United States that discretion is vested in courts. The differences in the degree of discretion and in the control of discretion in the adjudication of cases seem slight.

Discretion with respect to initiating an enforcement proceeding is much broader and much less controlled, both in Europe and in America. The great discretionary power in both instances is the power not to enforce, either in general, against a class of parties, or against a particular party. And, of course, discretion not to enforce intrinsically involves discretion to discriminate—a power very dangerous to justice.

On the basis of Mr. Meessen's excellent analysis of the system in the European Communities, I cannot determine that the Europeans handle that kind of discretion better than the Americans do, but my wondering—perhaps my leaning—is in that direction. During a ten-year period, the average number of European cases initiated was twenty each year. The number was small because of a limited staff, because the investigatory procedure lacks efficiency, and because of a deliberately cautious policy. What seems especially significant is that the Commission in 1963 adopted a resolution containing principles for the selection of cases, although selection was not merely about complaints but was about applications, notifications, and complaints. On the basis of the regulation, selections were made, and the selections were used as precedents. The Commission followed the plan to decide cases of different categories so as to use them as precedents. Then large numbers of cases were terminated informally on the basis of decisions in test cases.

The weak spot in the European system is apparently not in cases in which decisions are made to take action against a violator, but in cases in which decisions are made not to take such action. The affirmative decision is reviewed by at least twenty officers with university degrees, but the negative decision rests mainly with the individual official and comes to the attention of only a small number of officials. Mr. Meessen explicitly says he was unable to determine whether the power to delay has ever been abused. The European system may thus provide less than adequate protection against possible abuse of the discretionary power not to enforce.

But the system of the Antitrust Division of the U.S. Department of Justice may be more deficient in that respect. The discretionary power of nonenforcement is enormous and little protected. No one outside the Department of Justice supervises or reviews decisions not to investigate or decisions not to prosecute. Such negative decisions are secretly made. No systematic reporting of them to anyone is required. The officers who make the decisions may have private conferences with parties under

Ex parte influence on prosecutors.

investigation, and those parties do not always limit their presentations to facts and arguments; they may use influence of various kinds—influence that is typically known only to the officers with whom they are dealing. The potential for abuse is almost unlimited. If abuse occurs, the possibility of its detection or correction is slight, usually almost nonexistent.

A congressional investigation into possible abuse of the power to withhold an antitrust prosecution was made in 1972 on the occasion of Senate confirmation of the nomination of Richard Kleindeinst as Attorney General. The nominee had participated in a conference with the International Telephone and Telegraph Company on a question of possible prosecution of the company for antitrust violation. The conference was secret; the press and the public were prevented from criticizing. The Department of Justice made no findings, wrote no reasoned opinion, and was unchecked by any other authority except for the unusual congressional investigation. The charge that the non-prosecution decision was based in part on a political contribution was unproved.

The Antitrust Division has no regulation comparable to the 1963 regulation of the Commission of the European Communities. The closest approach is a 1968 set of merger guidelines in rather vague terms.

One top officer of the Antitrust Division once took a public position that his own prosecuting discretion should be confined by rules and by precedents. He said in the 1938 *Annual Report of the United States Attorney General:*

> An important part of our task is to facilitate compliance with the laws by helping conscientious businessmen to understand them. . . . Not only judicial policy but prosecution policy must be developed by precedent on publicly stated grounds if it is to clarify the law. . . . Businessmen are entitled to know what kinds of situations will lead to prosecution. . . . In consequence, on May 18, 1938, the policy was adopted of publishing explanatory statements in connection with each important step taken in the administration of the antitrust laws. These statements are intended cumulatively to formulate a consistent antitrust policy (pp. 59–60).

The Department followed through on the system for only two years, when it was cut off by World War II. Such a system could be worked out and followed today—either in America or in Europe.

CHAPTER FOUR

Enforcement of the Nuisance Act in the Netherlands

A. A. M. F. STAATSEN

INTRODUCTION

The Nuisance Act, which became effective in 1953, creates a system of licensing for "enterprises which can cause outside danger, damage or nuisance."

The subject of this inquiry is enforcement of this Act as an example of administrative discretion. The statute does not grant discretionary power in regard to enforcement, but the administrative practice assumes such power. My objectives are to describe the exercise of discretion from a legal point of view, and to evaluate it in terms of the quality of justice.

With that purpose in mind I had a series of interviews with administrators from four municipalities (out of about 850). Municipality A had about 10,000 enterprises governed by the Nuisance Act; B, about 2,500; C, about 2,000; and D, about 600. The municipalities for this inquiry are randomly selected. I interviewed the heads of the Nuisance Act Offices for A and D; the head of B's office and one of his subordinate enforcement officers; and two enforcement officers and a legal adviser of C. For the interviews I used a list of open-ended questions. During each interview I took notes from which I later prepared a report; I discussed my report with the officers interviewed and, when necessary, I corrected and amplified it. I had twelve interviews averaging three hours in length.

THE LEGAL FRAMEWORK

According to the explanatory memorandum accompanying it, the Nuisance Act is designed "to prevent enterprises from causing danger, damage or nuisance." The Act prohibits any unlicensed building or working which can cause outside danger, damage, or nuisance. A regulation of the central government designates which industries are governed by the Nuisance Act. The statutory sanctions involve closing down the enterprise and fining or imprisoning the violator. The statute provides: "When an enterprise works without a license or with an insufficient license or violates a provision of the license . . . it is wholly or partly closed down." The word "is" seems to be the equivalent of "shall be" in English or American law. If the legislative purpose had been to grant discretionary power to the administrators, the word "is" would have been "can be" or "may be." Imposing the sanction of closing down the enterprise is thus mandatory, according to the language of the statute. The competent authority (*i.e.,* the governing authority of the municipality) has no discretionary power to withhold enforcement by closing down the business that violates the statute. Imprisonment for not more than thirty days or a fine of not more than 3,000 guilders is also mandatory, but these sanctions are imposed by a judge, not by the administration.

That the legislature intended the sanctions to be mandatory is shown by the explanatory memorandum, which states that the government sets a high value on maintaining the obligation to close down the enterprise for a violation "in order to prevent officials from conniving with enterprises that are operating without licenses or committing other violations"; it even says that, in absence of this obligation, "the keystone of the system would lose its force." One Member of Parliament suggested that closing down an enterprise should be discretionary for cases involving no danger or nuisance, and that closing down should be mandatory only after a warning time. But the government rejected his proposal, referring to the possibility of review for the violator on the one hand and to the eventual harmful consequences for the environment on the other. "An extra warning, however, is not contrary to the spirit of the statute," the responsible minister added. In a circular letter eight years later the government advised that sanctions should be withheld until warning is given, allowing a reasonable time to comply, and that the enterprise should be closed down only if it refuses compliance. So the mandatory sanction does have some flexibility, according to the official statement.

Further indication that the power to close down an enterprise is mandatory appears in statements by the Crown as a reviewing agency: ". . . the enterprise operating without a required license must be closed down." That statement was made in 1967. In the Gulf Oil case of 1972 the Crown spoke of "the mandatory character" of the statute. Upon finding a violation, the administration has the obligation to impose the sanction, except that the sanction may be delayed until a violation occurs after a warning. The judge also has a mandatory duty to impose a penalty of fine or imprisonment, but he has discretion about the extent of the penalty, which may be very slight.

COMPETENCE AND ORGANIZATION

The Executive of the local government has the competent authority to close down an enterprise, but non-compliance first has to be found. Enforcement officers assigned by the executive are charged with investigating violations. For the administration of the Nuisance Act only (licensing and enforcement) seventeen officers are available in A, four in B, three in C, and two in D. In addition, especially in A, other officers of the Building Department report simple violations of the Nuisance Act.

Although complaints are made and violations are established almost daily, enterprises are closed down in B and D only about twice a year, and not at all during the last few years in A and C.

PROCEDURE

The closing down is executed by means of a written determination, preceded by a written notice of intention to close down. However, in cases involving a danger to life or intolerable nuisance, an enterprise can be closed immediately. The Criminal Procedure Code offers the necessary provisions as to the procedure used in the application of sanctions by the criminal judge.

Inquiries into a possible violation are sometimes initiated by the administrators, but usually by a private complainant. Complaints may be made in writing, in person, or by telephone. If necessary, the inspector visits the complainant to gather information about the nature of the complaint. He establishes the nature of the nuisance and then visits the enterprise. If he finds no violation, he notifies the complainant. In B a complaint is considered settled only when the answer has been approved by the office head. Even if there is no statutory violation, the resulting nuisance may still be unacceptable, and the officer may institute a proceeding to modify the license. Rarely, a private party may apply to the Executive for a change in the provisions of a license.

If a violation is found, the officer confers with the management of the enterprise or with its technical department in an effort to get a voluntary cessation of the nuisance. If the enterprise does not have the license required by the Nuisance Act, or has only an insufficient one, the officer requires it to apply for a license. All agreements between the officer and the enterprise (e.g., relating to the measures to be taken or the ultimate date for the termination of the nuisance) are noted informally. The enterprise may receive a written confirmation, depending upon the nature of the violation and the attitude of the violator, but not a formal written agreement.

If the violator promises to comply with the requirements, the complainant is notified, and the officer may ask the complainant to notify him if the nuisance has not ceased within a given time. If the business is unlicensed or insufficiently licensed, the complainant is informed that the business will be required to obtain a proper license. In that case the opportunity to enter objections in due time is pointed out to the complainant.

If the enterprise fails to comply with the requirements, it is exhorted verbally in terms of the possible consequences of its noncompliance. If necessary the head of the office is involved.

If verbal exhortations are in vain, the enterprise will receive a letter from the head of the department warning that, unless the requirements are fulfilled, he will advise the Executive to close it down. Only in cases of obstinate refusal does the department so advise the Executive. The Executive thereupon notifies the violator in writing of its intention. To gain time, the violator may ask for a review, thus temporarily suspending further execution. If not, or after review, the notification may be followed by the actual closing down. The advice to the Executive to close down the business contains findings and reasons but is not open to the public. The notification of the intended closing down is sent to the licensee or to the manager of the enterprise, indicating the provisions violated and stating that the violator did not comply in spite of repeated exhortations. It also points out the possibility of an appeal to the Crown and the fact that such an appeal suspends the execution of the closing down. In case of a closing down because of danger to life or intolerable nuisance, the appeal does *not* suspend the execution and is therefore not mentioned in the notification. The complainant is informed, but his legal possibilities for a review are not pointed out to him, because he is not entitled to take an appeal. During each stage of this procedure the officer may decide to draw up an official record of the violation for the prosecutor, who has discretionary power to decide whether or not to prosecute.

The complainant plays only a minor role in the procedure; he is unable to check the course of the complaint, and he cannot take an administrative appeal. To strengthen the position of the complainant I would consider the following measures to be desirable. First, every oral complaint should be affirmed in writing. As not every complaint results in an investigation, the complainant should have a better means of checking the progress of the inquiry. If the investigation reveals nothing wrong or nothing that can be done, the complainant should be notified in writing, with reasons, and should be told what action he can take if he does not accept the conclusion. The complainant should be notified in writing of all agreements and should be kept informed of the progress of the case. It is clear that if the local administration were to act more strictly in accordance with the statute, better protection for those who are suffering from illegal nuisances caused by industry would result.

In order to clarify the position of the enterprise whenever a violation is found, the enterprise should be notified in writing, stating the findings, the needed action, the termination date for such action, and the appeal procedure.

RULES AND RULEMAKING

Despite the mandatory sanctions prescribed by the Nuisance Act, sanctions are not always imposed when violations are established. One enforcement officer said, "It is not my duty to close enterprises but to prevent or to eliminate nuisances." Officers usually believe they can most effectively eliminate nuisances by maintaining good relations with the businessmen. Closing down a business may be too strong a measure; correcting the violation may be better. Yet violations may continue while the procedure for closing down is operating. The delay may be over a long period.

Enforcement officers have to decide when to investigate, when to confer with managers, what measures to require at once, whether to disregard some violations, whether to be content with half measures or to sternly require complete measures, whether to demand expensive measures or to accept cheaper ones that are less effective, and how long to allow for compliance. They decide whether and when to advise the Executive to proceed to close down the business, and they decide whether and when to ask a prosecutor to start a criminal proceeding.

In all this, the enforcement officers are unguided by explicit rules, except that the *Nuisance Act Handbook,* composed and edited by the Association of Nuisance Act Administrators, deals with the policy of licensing and with attaching prescriptions to licenses.

Practices vary. Some investigations are made irregularly and some periodically. Usually an investigation follows a complaint, but sometimes a complainant is told to contact the enterprise directly. When a violation is found, the officer gets in touch with the manager. One who operates without a license may be told to apply for one at once, but nothing further may be done unless a nuisance is caused. For instance, a shoemaker with machines of less than two horsepower need not have a license, but he may need one if he buys new machines with more power. If he does not know he needs a license, he is not penalized if the machines do not cause a nuisance, but he is required to get a license.

Even when the statute requires a license, the *Handbook* suggests overlooking the violation in a "minimum case" involving a small violation. "In the case of a Nuisance Act minimum we may be tolerant unless we receive a complaint," one officer said. And "incidental violations" may be overlooked, such as incidental storage of goods where they should not be.

To eliminate a nuisance the officer may demand use of a better installation, such as burning refuse in an incinerator instead of in a heater. To purify gases evaporating from snack bars, the officer may require an expensive device that washes the air but requires regular checking, or he may accept a simple grease filter that is less expensive but less effective.

The time allowed for compliance varies. Illegal storage of propane within the town is dangerous and requires immediate action. When a complete rebuilding is necessary, more time may be allowed, unless a decision is made to close down. Threats are sometimes appropriate: "If you don't stop repairing cars at night, we will close down your garage." The attitude of the violator may determine the severity of the action. Imposing sanctions is usually a last resort—"The closing down is labor lost. One proceeds to this only if the violator deliberately refuses to cooperate and the nuisance is serious."

The officer balances the interests of the enterprise against those of the complaining neighbors; he may also take into account the unemployment that results from closing down an enterprise.

The leniency policies are neither governed by rules nor stated in writing. Officers in B even acknowledge that each officer has his own methods, which may differ in each area and even from one enterprise to another. An officer in D says: "One time you may be more flexible than another. Your mood plays an important role. The officer's tolerance varies." In B, C, and D, the small size of the organization allows discussions that tend to minimize differences. In A, special attention is given to instructing officers through discussing specific cases.

Rulemaking on enforcement policy is possible, but it is not likely to be easy, because the range of subjects is wide and the variety of situations is almost unlimited. But in D there is an unwritten rule that purchasers of rags who usually sell them on the same day do not need a license; the rule could be written. A rule could provide that storage of propane without a license is not permitted in a town, and that a violator will be closed down immediately. A rule could state that a business which dumps garbage illegally will be closed down after one warning. Cases could be described in which criminal prosecution will be requested.

Most existing unwritten rules can be turned into written rules, yet most officers believe rules are unnecessary. They say that problems differ from case to case, that rules would have to be changed frequently, that they would impede a flexible administration and that they would not be useful.

Despite the mandatory duty created by the statute, officers assume a discretionary power which can be exercised in various ways. The *Nuisance Act Handbook* could act as an influence toward uniformity, but it says very little about enforcement.

Officers in C believe that rules about enforcement could be useful, and I am inclined to agree with them. Rules need not be inflexible and need not impede a flexible policy. Rules can allow deviation to a reasonable extent and need not be a hindrance in deciding difficult questions. The gap between what the statute prescribes and the practices of the officers causes serious legal insecurity to both private parties and officers.

The reason given in C for not formulating written rules is that the enforcement policy is not in accordance with the statute; the officers fear that, in deciding appeals, the Crown would decide that the statute has priority over the rules. But such officers forget that unwritten rules can likewise be reviewed by the Crown, as shown by the case of Gulf Oil Refining Company v. The Municipality of Rozenburg, upholding an order closing down a refinery that was operating without a license. The Crown criticized the Executive: "The Executive tolerated the operation without a license." Any conflict between the statute and the enforcement practices should be decided ultimately by the competent reviewing authority, the Crown.

OPENNESS

The enforcement policy cannot be open and accessible unless it is written. Only those who attend a hearing during the license proceeding receive copies of the determination and can consequently know the provisions with which the enterprise must comply. They can check the extent to which an enterprise complies with the law and the extent to which the enforcement officers are deficient. The annual reports of the municipalities do not contain significant information, but perhaps they should.

In A, publicity is used as a sanction against violators. The officers give the press information about violations. Such publicity is effective against those whose customers are in the local community, and sometimes it can be quite effective in inducing prompt compliance. Some officers say that rules should not be open, because businesses will use to the utmost every nonenforcement possibility, but my opinion is that using a strict law along with a lenient and secret enforcement policy is unjust.

CHECKING

An enterprise that receives a notice that it is closed down may appeal to the Crown; the order is then suspended pending the appeal, except in a case of danger to life or intolerable nuisance. Administrators of the central government can appeal to the Crown from a refusal to close down an enterprise. A private party other than the enterprise has no right of appeal, but he should have, especially because of the gap between the strict enforcement provided by the statute and the lenient enforcement that is customary. When a prosecutor makes a decision not to prosecute, a party who seeks prosecution is entitled to take an appeal to the court.

In day-to-day practice, an enforcement officer is almost never supervised. He works independently and discusses only difficult cases with his superiors. People who disagree with action or inaction of enforcement officers may turn to the Executive, and supervision of officers may take place when a complaint is registered.

CONCLUSIONS

Many people are complaining of the gap between statutory strictness and enforcement leniency. The gap could be closed by changing the statute to make the power of closing down an industry discretionary. The statute could also indicate some situations in which an enterprise must be closed down (*e.g.,* danger, intolerable nuisance, or willful violations) and could indicate other circumstances when an enterprise may be closed down in the absence of compliance after notice. Perhaps sanctions could be added to the two present ones of closing down and fine or imprisonment. In addition, rules might be formulated to enlarge the rights of one who is complaining of a nuisance.

American Comments on Dutch Nuisance Act Enforcement

Americans who have been exposed to the system of the German prosecutor may wonder whether other enforcement officers in Europe are denied the kind of discretionary power that Americans customarily allow their enforcement officers to exercise. Mr. Staatsen's study of enforcement of the Nuisance Act in the Netherlands provides an answer with respect to the one small sample. The answer, in broad terms, is that Dutch enforcement officers do in fact exercise discretionary power that the literal words of the statute and of the legislative history do not fully support, and yet I think the discretion is probably more limited and controlled than it would be in the United States.

Much discretionary power of administrative officers in the United States is unplanned by legislative bodies and grows up despite the lack of any grant of such power. American legislative bodies generally have conferred no discretionary power upon either police or prosecutors, and yet the reality is that both police and prosecutors exercise enormous discretionary power which is neither limited nor guided by statutes and which is generally unguided either by statutory standards or by administrative rules. American legislative bodies characteristically look the other way; they have not granted the uncontrolled discretionary power, but they seem to acquiesce when the administrators assume such power.

The story of enforcement of the Nuisance Act in the Netherlands has a close resemblance to what happens in America, but with some differences. The Dutch Parliament did not confer upon enforcement officers a discretionary power to be lenient, but from the beginning officers have exercised such discretionary power. The statute, as Mr. Staatsen analyzes it on the basis of his understanding of Dutch statutory interpretation, makes enforcement mandatory in all circumstances—except that, when the danger is not immediate, the officer may give a warning and withhold the sanction unless the violation continues or is repeated after the warning. The only nonenforcement discretion, according to Mr. Staatsen, is limited to the question of whether to impose the sanction at once or whether to give a warning first.

Yet the enforcement officers do in fact exercise much more discretionary power than that. Officers balance the interests of the enterprise against those of the complaining neighbors; in so doing they even take into account the unemployment that may result from closing down a business. Degrees of leniency creep in all along the line. As Mr. Staatsen describes it, the gap between the statutory strictness and the enforcement leniency is in fact a substantial one.

My American point of view about the probable intent of the Dutch Parliament tends to differ from Mr. Staatsen's. Even in the light of the legislative history he emphasizes, I am inclined to believe that the legislative intent may have been quite consistent with the enforcement system which the officers are in fact providing. True, the words state explicitly that enforcement is mandatory, except for the leniency in first giving notice. But sophisticated members of the Dutch Parliament must have known from experience with other statutes that the realities of enforcement are likely to differ from what is said in the formal legislative materials. Parliament can choose the strictest enforcement policy, or a middle one, or the most lenient one. Whichever one it chooses, and no matter how clearly it expresses its choice, it knows that what the officers will produce is likely to be only about 80 percent of what the legislative words say. The choice of the strictest policy rather than the middle one still has a great deal of meaning, because 80 percent of the strictest one might be the equivalent of 100 percent of the middle one.

Some discretionary play in the joints may be intrinsic to *any* enforcement system—European or American—and legislators probably should legislate with that knowledge. *If* the Dutch Parliament legislated with such knowledge, as I assume it must have, then I think the interpreters of the statute should interpret with such knowledge. Therefore, my own conclusion is that the present enforcement policies are not generally at variance with the true parliamentary intent; the words used, literally interpreted, call for stricter enforcement than the officers have provided, but the true intent may have been that the officers should do about what they have done.

Perhaps in arriving at that conclusion I am conditioned by my American background, which includes knowledge of long-term acquiescence of American legislators in long-term violations by police and prosecutors and other enforcement officers of the statutory words requiring full enforcement. When American legislators provide that their statutes "shall" be enforced, they generally mean that the enforcement officers are intended to have considerable discretionary power not to enforce. Something much more than a mere "shall" or the word "duty" is necessary if the real intent is to depart from the traditional power of enforcement officers to provide some degree of nonenforcement.

All American states but New Mexico have full enforcement statutes, typically providing that every policeman has a duty to enforce all criminal legislation, and sometimes providing penalties for policemen who fail to enforce all such legislation. But for more than a century American police have been providing far less than full enforcement, and the legislators have acquiesced. Indeed, the acquiescence may be a much better indication of the true legislative intent than the literal words of the full enforcement legislation, for the acquiescence is backed up by the appropriation of only enough for half or two-thirds of full enforcement. American legislators provide for full enforcement with the knowledge that full enforcement will be interpreted to mean something much less than that.

My opinion is that American legislators could provide for a better system if they would say what they mean and mean what they say, but my opinion also is that that is not what they have done. Indeed, the evidence is overwhelming, I think, that, in enacting criminal legislation, American legislators are accustomed to rely on police and prosecutors to cut back the excessive provisions; the legislators know that they can err on the side of including too much and that the enforcement officers will whittle down what they make criminal, so that the result will be a sensible one. When legislators for more than a century have used words of full enforcement without meaning what they say, one who seeks their true intent must be careful not to give literal meaning to words that are not intended to be interpreted literally. Dutch legislators seem to have some resemblance to American legislators in that respect.

After all, as pointed out in my commentary on Professor Herrmann's essay on German prosecutors, the federal statute governing U.S. attorneys, 28 U.S.C. § 547, provides that the U.S. attorney "shall" prosecute for "all" offenses, but the system clearly is that "shall" means "may" and "all" means "some." United States v. Cox, 342 F.2d 167, 171 (5th Cir. 1965), certiorari denied.

An incidental reason for my tendency to disagree with Mr. Staatsen's view that the enforcement officers are violating the legislative intent is limited to the imposition of the criminal penalties. Because the Dutch prosecutor traditionally has discretionary power to refrain from prosecuting for minor crimes, I think the Dutch Parliament must have legislated in the light of that tradition; it must have intended less than full enforcement of the criminal penalties. For instance, if a shoemaker's machine is over the two horsepower limit, if his refusal to get a license is a clear violation, but if the prosecutor refrains from prosecuting him because he is old and feeble, because no one is complaining, and because the prosecutor sympathizes with his individualism, I think the prosecutor is not violating the parliamentary intent. After all, does not the traditional prosecutorial discretion exist unless Parliament does something to negative it? And if the prosecutor may refrain from prosecuting, may not the enforcement officer refrain from requesting a prosecution?

I strongly agree with Mr. Staatsen that officers who enforce the Dutch Nuisance Act should formulate rules to clarify their enforcement policies. The main purpose of the rules should be to govern the degree of leniency in various circumstances—that is, the circumstances in which nonenforcement is appropriate. I think a nonenforcement rule that would violate Mr. Staatsen's interpretation of the statute would be perfectly legal. For instance, a rule could provide: "When a violation is not dangerous to life and has only a minor effect upon the complaining parties and upon others, when the costs of full compliance are high, and when closing down the business will throw a large number of employees out of work, the officers shall balance one set of interests against the other and make a discretionary determination of whether or not to close down the enterprise."

Mr. Staatsen's interpretation of the statute apparently would preclude such a rule, yet he favors enforcement rules. I doubt that a good set of enforcement rules could be formulated unless the statute is interpreted to allow the kind of limited nonenforcement that is now in fact provided by the officers.

My opinion is that the enforcement practices described by Mr. Staatsen are probably broadly in agreement with the true legislative intent. Those practices can and should be captured in a set of rules governing enforcement, but the rules should be drafted to continue discretionary power to do the needed individualizing.

CHAPTER FIVE

The Family Guidance Center
in Copenhagen

LARS BUSCK

This study deals with grants of money by the Family Guidance
Center in Copenhagen. These grants are over and above the
social security benefits administered through other programs.
The program of special grants has grown out of an earlier
program that was limited to family counseling.

The principal means of getting information for this study
has been through interviews with the various administrators
at the Family Guidance Center, as well as at the Danish
Ministry of Social Affairs and at other social agencies. The research has also included attendance at various administrative
group conferences and the study of written accounts of individual cases, as well as written rules, principles, and policy
statements.

THE PROGRAM OF FAMILY GUIDANCE

Welfare benefits in Denmark include both money and services;
the services include institutional care, counseling, and treatment. The main portion of the money grants in other programs
are guided by fixed criteria such as income, capital, disease,
birth, unemployment, age, and marital status, but discretionary
determinations still must depend upon evaluation of the need
for assistance. Providing guidance for families with children
usually involves a greater range for discretion. The objective
of rehabilitating families requires highly individualized appraisals of economic, social, and psychological facts.

The family guidance service began in 1964. A main original objective was to coordinate the multiplicity of assistance measures—to provide a unified effort for the client, on the basis of an overall evaluation of his need for various kinds of help. A central task was to provide practical and personal guidance in the care of the children, the housekeeping, the economy of the family, and (to some extent) the vocational and legal problems.

Out of the system of counseling has grown the system of providing special money benefits which supplement those for which the family may be eligible under other programs. Money benefits administered by the Family Guidance Center are thus tailored to the unique needs of a particular family. Discretion accordingly has to be broad and little confined.

The Children and Young Persons Act of 1964 provided in § 18: "The child and youth welfare committee may offer families with children continuing guidance and support and shall be required to make such offer to families who are supposed to be in particular need thereof." In the larger municipalities, family guidance centers have been established for serving the approximately 250 local communities. Most centers have expanded within the last few years, including the one in Copenhagen, which is the largest.

The Minister of Social Affairs has statutory authority to issue regulations. He has general supervisory authority, and he decides certain administrative appeals. Also at the central level is the National Council of Child and Youth Welfare Services, which is the general administrative appeals authority for decisions of the local child and youth welfare committees. The Council decides appeals in specific cases; it has no authority to issue general instructions to the local agencies. The Council reviews decisions of the Family Guidance Center; the Council's decisions are not reviewable by any other administrative authority, except that the Minister of Social Affairs may review a local agency's denial of assistance. The Minister has never reviewed such a decision of the FGC.

THE FAMILY GUIDANCE CENTER (FGC) IN COPENHAGEN

The supreme authority in Copenhagen is the third division of Magistraten, made up of three directorates each under a director, a secretariat, and headed by the Mayor of Social Affairs. Amounts up to 1,500 kroner can be granted by a director or his assistant, but larger amounts can be granted only by the Mayor. Amounts up to 1,000 kroner are granted by office heads, and up to 500 by other officers, including lawyers of the service. Any decision by a subordinate may be changed by his superior in the organization.

The FGC, by far the largest office, is a more or less independent unit within the administrative pyramid; its public image is more favorable than that of some other offices. The FGC employs about a hundred persons, half of whom are called family counselors and work in the field. The other half work at the office of the Center. Each of eight units has six to eight counselors, with a back-up team and a clerical staff.

The FGC serves about 1,200 families during each year for periods of varying length, but it decides between 2,000 and 3,000 applications each year; a single family may make several applications. The average service period for one family is a little more than a year. About three-quarters of those who receive service also receive economic grants. Only about 5 percent of applications for such grants are denied.

Family counselors all have three months of education in common, in addition to their experience as nurses, youth center administrators, or schoolteachers. A few, mostly young, have college degrees in social work, but some of the middle-aged women have no specialized education other than the three months of training. The family counselors visit clients in their homes; they are the key workers in the service, and they have the main influence on decisions involving money grants.

Each supervisor has about seven family counselors working under him. A supervisor is required to have a college degree in social work and some practical experience. Each of the eight groups (supervisor and counselors) meets once a week. One special group, made up of counselors with college degrees and including a back-up team of lawyer, psychologist, and psychiatrist, performs the intake function, with conferences of at least one hour per day. The back-up team also gives advice to the other groups. The seven lawyers have exclusive legal authority to make money grants, and the seven of them as a group have power to issue general instructions.

The statute provides in § 27: "It shall be the duty of the child and youth welfare committee to give guidance to [the parent] where it appears that the breadwinner is unable to provide for the child in a proper manner, that the child has difficulty adjusting to his daily environment or his school, that the child is not properly cared for, or that otherwise the child is exposed to unsatisfactory conditions of living. In such cases the committee may resolve . . . to make grants to meet temporary difficulties to obviate the need for removing the child from the home." The power to make grants is the fifth of six enumerated powers, and the sixth is "to arrange for the child to be accommodated apart from his parents" in an educational or therapeutic institution. The five requisites for a money grant are (1) a family with at least one child under 18 who is exposed to unsatisfactory conditions, (2) difficulties which are temporary, (3) a need for removing the child from the home, (4) need for assistance, and (5) the money grant must be an integral part of continuing general guidance and support. Other statutory provisions guiding money grants are relatively vague.

STATUTORY LIMITS ON DISCRETION

Although the general purpose of the grants is broadly stated, and although the five requisites for a grant are specified, the statute does not fix a maximum amount for any grant, and it contains no provision governing the amount to be provided in any case. Each of the five requisites is undefined and imprecise. The discretionary power delegated by the statute is thus enormous. By liberal interpretation of the five requisites, almost any normal home with one or more children would qualify; by strict interpretation, hardly any such home would qualify. The statutory limits on discretion are indeed far out. Yet the term "temporary difficulties" creates an important restriction which gives the whole program a very distinctive character: the many families whose difficulties seem to be permanent are excluded. The purpose of the money grant must be to lift the family through a limited time period; the prospect must be that the family that is helped for a brief period will then be able to take care of itself. Yet the statute does not define "temporary"; it does not say whether the statute is violated by providing private day care for a child for a period having no foreseeable end date. But the liberality of the administrators has not been legislatively disapproved. The appropriations and the vague statutory terms continue. The actual need of a family, as appraised subjectively by the administrators, fixes the outer limits of the program of granting money. Other welfare programs are much more rule-oriented than this one.

COUNSELING

Family guidance is designed to provide help to families with any temporary difficulties concerning bringing up the children, the school, housekeeping, employment, housing, health, the budget, and intrafamily relationships. The purpose is to help the family through a difficult period so that they may then independently take care of themselves. The counseling is primarily practical, and grants are one facet of the whole task of resolving difficulties.

Families themselves usually initiate the process by telephoning or coming to the FGC. About two-thirds of those who seek help are turned away—usually referred to other agencies; the crucial test is no more precise than "need for family guidance." A vital question is whether guidance is likely to solve the temporary problems.

The plan calls for taking care of each in about six months, but the reality averages more than a year. Very few cases are concluded in less than three months. Each family counselor has about twenty active cases at one time.

Most of the families that are beneficiaries of the service are at the lowest economic level, but of course affluent families may

also need counseling. Almost half of the clients are single
mothers with one child or more, and some are single fathers.
The average number of children in the client families is 2½,
compared with the national average of about 1½.

About 70–80 percent of family guidance cases involve money
grants. Some are less than 50 kroner and some are several
thousand kroner, the average being between 200 and 300. The
money is almost always for a specified purpose; a large portion
of it is used for day care of children. Other frequent items
include rent, installment payments, mortgages, and bills for
services or household items.

EXAMPLE

In October, 1970, a young mother of children three and four
years old asked for help. She had been married for four years
but sought separation from her husband, an unskilled worker
who was often drunk and, when drunk, was cruel to his wife
and children. She sought help in finding another place to live
and in getting her children into a nursery school. Shortly after
she applied, the husband committed suicide. The counselor
visited the home, a two-room apartment that was cold and un-
sanitary; the children constantly had colds, and one of them was
suffering from influenza. The nearest toilet was on the other
side of the street. The mother had tenosynovitis, feminine
troubles, and bad nerves. The family was getting 225 kroner
per week. The counselor recommended grants to pay for
laundry, because the mother was almost unable to do the
washing. The recommendation was for 20 kroner per week
for three months, a total of 250 kroner. That was granted, along
with 21 kroner for vitamin pills. The counselor then got the
children into a home for children; most of the expenses were
paid by other agencies, with whom the counselor made the
arrangements. The children stayed there for three months,
until the counselor found a place for them in a nursery school.
The mother found a job, and the counselor then found a new
apartment, in order to take the children out of the cold and
unhealthful apartment. The mother was able to pay the rent

from her wages, and the counselor helped the mother work out the family budget. A grant of 550 kroner was found necessary and was made. After a year and a half, the counselor made a final report that no more assistance and no more visits were needed.

Discretionary Grants of Money

A grant of money must be part of a plan for rehabilitating a family; the counselor, on the basis of all the facts and circumstances, must make a discretionary determination, subject to the check of the back-up team. The central element may be the personality, intellect, and feelings of the counselor, as well as the relationship that develops between the counselor and the family. In comparison with the impressions of the counselor and the human element in his relationship with the family, the rest of the administrative apparatus of the FGC—the rules, experts, group conferences, and formal decision structure—is of only secondary importance; all that apparatus is limited to a consultative or corrective role, whereas the counselor's reactions are usually decisive.

If the system goes wrong, the failure will almost always be that of the counselor, although the supervising apparatus may also fail to correct the counselor's failure. That the formal decision is made by the lawyer who is a part of the back-up team does not change the fact that the crucial determination is made by the counselor, for the lawyer seldom reverses or modifies the counselor's recommendations.

A counselor's negative decision—a decision not to make a money grant—may often be unreviewable in reality, for the counselor has the power to withhold from his report some of the facts that a member of the back-up team could regard as enough to support a money grant. Although there are no formal obstacles, a client can hardly ever take the initiative in informing the back-up team of facts that the counselor does not report, so the opportunity for a counselor's abuse of discretion in denying a grant is quite real. Abuse of discretion in improperly making grants or in providing excessive grants is much less likely, but instances of excessive grants can be found. Examples include a grant for redeeming a diamond ring pawned by a mother; the counselor found that the ring had much sentimental value, and that the mother's remorse at having pawned it was so great that the children's welfare required the mother to have the ring. Another example involves a family of foreign origin who had been mistreated and defrauded. They were supplied transportation money to return to their own country; the FGC was aware of their hidden savings, but made a political decision in their favor as a kind of compensation for the wrongs inflicted on them. A third example concerns support for a family's hot dog stand that was not economically viable; the grants merely postponed the collapse of the little business. In all three instances one may have some sympathy for the counselor's determinations, even though one may conclude in each instance that the grant should not have been made.

In other cases, decisions of counselors have been reversed. The following examples are based mostly on interviews; the officers believe that each case could be real.

Example 1. The father of four minor children has been unemployed; since he is not a member of a trade union, he is not entitled to unemployment benefits. Debts are piling up, creditors are making threats, and the children are suffering from violent arguments between the parents. The counselor, a middle-aged woman who in a similar family circumstance had taken a job as a maid, does not propose a grant of money but finds a job for the mother. She may have felt that the mother should not have benefits which she herself had not had. The superior officers say that this was a typical example of a case where money should be granted, and that the children's welfare required that the mother stay home with them.

Example 2. A foreign family with children pays unreasonably high rent to a landlord who takes advantage of foreigners. The young family counselor refuses a grant to the family because the money will go to the greedy landlord, instead referring the family to the agency for homeless persons, whose housing is unsatisfactory. The superior officers believe that this decision was wrong, because the paramount consideration should be the welfare of the family; a grant should have been made for the exorbitant rent until satisfactory housing could be found.

Example 3. The father drinks and mistreats his wife and two children when drunk. His wife loves him when he is sober, and so do the children, but they are becoming nervous because of disputes between the parents. The counselor, a woman who divorced her husband for excessive drinking, recommended a separation that was opposed by the man and recommended a money grant to the mother and children, who were cut off from the man's income by the separation. The officers say that the counselor should have been neutral between the parents and should not have used money to provide a solution which was unfavorable to one of them.

RULES

The minister in 1966 issued a forty-page set of instructions on child care services, dealing mostly with organization and procedure, and only to a slight extent with guides for discretion. Similarly, 1971 instructions add very little to the statutory guides. Example: "The aim of the family assistance work is to help the family manage the momentary difficulties and, as far as possible, to enable it to take care of future problems by its own means."

The instructions have been published in an official paper called *Ministerialtidende,* but no FGC clients ever read this paper. The instructions theoretically bind the administrators, but no problem of their interpretation has ever arisen in a reviewing court. The key fact is that the instructions almost never answer questions that arise in individual cases.

An officer in the Ministry who handles child welfare services wrote an article, in a semi-private monthly publication, which dealt with discretion in making money grants for child welfare. The article compared various economic assistance measures and found the benefits administered by FGC the most generous, because those benefits may provide for the welfare of the children by going beyond the usual maximum of preserving the previous standard of living. Perhaps the most valuable part of the article is the discussion of real cases. Example: A man with income inadequate to pay his debts is granted 1,200 kroner, and a budget is drawn up for him to follow so that he can pay the rest, with the result that a harmonious family life is re-established. The mention of specific amounts can be a guide for discretion in similar cases, as some administrators have asserted. Perhaps the reception of the article shows a need for further guidance from the Ministry. Concrete examples may serve as better guides than abstract formulations in the form of instructions or rules.

The FGC itself has a chaotic mass of written statements, including social-political declarations, procedural and organizational arrangements, and policy formulations. Determining which such statements should be called "rules" is difficult. Few rules, in the sense of statements to govern or guide decisions, have been issued. The Mayor and the Director rarely issue instructions to the FGC, but a few do exist, including: (1) the FGC may not make money grants except in a context of family guidance; (2) decisions should be based on "correct and indisputable information"; (3) the FGC should show restraint in supporting a large consumption of tobacco or stimulants; (4) private day care may be supported for a child not eligible for public day care, but the maximum is 110 kroner per week.

The four instructions are the only ones in "The Collection" —a compilation distributed to all superior officers. "The Collection" contains three selected cases. One explains reasons for rejecting a request to raise payments for day care to 130 kroner. Another denies support for a baby sitter, without stating reasons. The third is a detailed account of complex facts in a case upholding a denial of a grant; the case provides general guidance as to what kind of considerations are relevant. "The Collection" also contains references to eighteen cases dealing with grants to apprentices with children. "The Collection" is probably open to inspection to anyone who asks to see it, but no one remembers such a request.

When the Mayor makes comments in deciding whether or not to approve a grant of more than 1,000 kroner, his comments may be regarded as an internal rule at the FGC. The FGC has recently decided to make a systematic collection of such comments, but the comments have more to do with economizing than with how to provide equal justice. The Director meets with senior officers of the FGC once a month to discuss policies, and some remarks are included in "The Collection."

Every Thursday, all FGC lawyers meet for an hour with the head of the FGC. The conference seems to be the supreme authority at FGC—at least with respect to economic grants. Each lawyer keeps a book of conference reports. Specific problems are discussed, and decisions appear in a weekly newspaper called *Avisen,* which has become the common means of written communication at FGC. *Avisen* contains matters of general professional interest, jokes, contributions on personnel matters and procedural problems, and a continuing discussion of administrative policies. It contains rules and guidelines of varying kinds. *Avisen* seems to have superseded other means of communicating internal instructions. All employees at FGC contribute to *Avisen,* and all keep copies of it. Copies of *Avisen* are open to inspection by outsiders, but no one asks for it.

Decisions of the meetings of lawyers that might guide discretion are included in *Avisen.* Guides for decisions include: (1) a statement of requisites for grants for moving (to another local community); (2) a statement concerning use of a private assistance association for making repairs in homes, with the costs paid by FGC; (3) grants for children of apprentices who have not completed their training and cannot support themselves or the children; (4) a rule that unemployed foreign workers shall be treated exactly the same way as Danish unemployed workers; (5) a rule that income of a child who receives a disability pension must be included as a part of the family budget for purposes of determining money grants to the family.

A thorough and extensive study of *Avisen* is necessary to get a general idea of what considerations are relevant in making grants. One may learn those considerations much more quickly by talking with any of the officers at the FGC.

OPENNESS

The Danish Information Act of 1970 allows inspection of files of cases but exempts from disclosure "information on personal and economic matters relating to individual persons" and "internal working documents of the agency." The meaning of the last phrase is unclear. Probably rules, guidelines, policy statements, and any other document in the nature of law should be open to public inspection. Since no one asks for such materials, perhaps the FGC should take the initiative in announcing that all such materials are available on request.

Perhaps one essential for justice, since the FGC ordinarily limits aid to those who apply for it, is that FGC should publicize the availability of aid to those who are eligible. Otherwise, those who are entitled to aid are denied it on account of their own ignorance.

The child welfare directorate publishes a small pamphlet called "For the Family," which is distributed free of charge by social agencies. Anyone may pick it up. But it leaves the impression of a very limited access to grants; the realities at FGC are quite different. A similar pamplet that will provide a more accurate impression of the realities is needed.

At one time FGC relied on reports from the National Registration Office of families that may be in need of assistance, but FGC found the number so large that the arrangement was not continued. One may surmise that if all who are entitled to benefits were to seek them, the system might collapse.

Today the most important publicizing of the program probably involves speeches by FGC officers in schools, hospitals, other social institutions, and meetings of social workers, along with some minor articles in professional publications.

The Information Act entitles a client to see all documents relating to his own case, except that the exemption of "internal working documents" applies. The result is that evaluations and recommendations are secret, but factual information is open to the client. The Information Act has made almost no change in practices, because only four or five applications have been made under the Act.

Procedure

An intake officer who accepts a case for investigation opens a file, and the case goes to the special group performing the intake function. A family counselor then visits the family; a report of each visit goes into the file. By the time the counselor makes a recommendation, the various reports may need to be integrated and summarized. The counselor follows a written instruction prepared by FGC lawyers and published in *Avisen* on "How to make a good and complete recommendation for assistance or refusal." The recommendation is usually discussed with the supervisor before it goes to the lawyer, who makes the decision. The lawyer sometimes asks for further information. If the amount of money is large enough, the decision moves up the hierarchy. A negative decision always goes as high as the head of FGC. More than 95 percent of all recommendations are positive, and more than 90 percent are accepted by the lawyer and his superiors, with modifications in very few.

The system of checking is quite effective, the only weak spot being the unchecked power of a counselor to omit from a report the facts that would support money grants that the counselor is not recommending. Even so, a family that is dissatisfied with a counselor may express the dissatisfaction, and the result may be the assignment of a new counselor. A client may complain directly to the lawyer responsible for the decision. Perhaps counselors who learn of such dissatisfaction should be required to tell clients about the availability of such procedures.

Although FGC is subordinate to both local and central officers, those officers do little supervising. The Minister may be consulted on questions of policy. Rarely does a case go to the National Appellate Board—only three or four a year out of about 2,000 decisions. Because the Mayor and the Director must approve the larger grants, some supervision results, and yet they usually approve decisions and rarely make comments. The Director meets with his office heads once a month, but such meetings do not influence decisions about grants. The

Director's attitude is that FGC performs well and needs no surveillance. No case from FGC has ever gone either to the ombudsman or to the courts, but the possibility of such procedure is always open.

GROUP WORK

Once a week for an hour the six or eight family counselors of each group meet with their supervisor. Each counselor meets individually with his supervisor once a week for a half-hour or more. Current cases are the main subject for discussion. In addition, supervisors may meet with individual counselors at other times.

All members of each group meet for an hour each week—the counselors, supervisor, lawyer, psychiatrist, and psychologist. Group conferences are the supreme authority about each case, but not all cases are considered by the group. Coordination conferences of members of more than one group, sometimes with representatives of other agencies or with other guests from the outside, are irregularly held as occasion arises.

Conferences of the seven lawyers are regularly held for an hour each week, to discuss general problems or specific cases. Records are kept, and extracts may be published in *Avisen,* but the records are usually not very extensive. Within the last three or four years, about ten accounts of cases dealing specifically with discretionary economic assistance have been so published. The conferences of the lawyers are especially important in that they coordinate the work of all parts of the FGC. Of course, some of the coordinating is done by the head of FGC, who attends many of the meetings, studies individual cases, and keeps himself available for consultation.

Other meetings include monthly meetings of all family counselors, monthly meetings of group supervisors, monthly meetings of all team members, and monthly meetings of office clerks, as well as weekly meetings of the office head, a psychologist, lawyer, supervisor, college-educated family counselor, ordinary family counselor, and an office clerk.

Another kind of group work contributing to the esprit de corps at the FGC is the vocational training courses and seminars. Besides the mandatory three-month training course for the new counselors, seminars on special subjects are held at irregular intervals, with the participation of all FGC officials or those particularly involved with the subject.

Altogether, group work is an outstanding characteristic of the FGC. A family counselor spends an average of an hour or more in meetings every day, and supervisors and team members may spend about three hours daily in meetings. The emphasis on group work produces a high level of common attitudes.

Indeed, because rules guide discretion to only a slight extent, perhaps the main force pulling toward equal justice within the FGC is the large amount of group work. Answers that cannot be found in any kind of written materials may often be highly crystallized in the living group mind of FGC. Newcomers learn how to make themselves a part of that group mind.

The deficiency in the heavy reliance upon group work may lie in inadequate recording. Valuable insights developed through group thinking strongly influence the behavior of participants who have them freshly in mind, but what happens to those insights through the passage of time? Recording is spotty and disorderly; "The Collection" is fragmentary and unsystematic; *Avisen* is uneven and inadequate. What is needed is a comprehensive recording of all ideas and experience that are worth preserving. The essence of the group thinking should be published in *Avisen,* and its files should be adequately indexed.

The costs of all the group work are exceedingly high, and the product is needlessly temporary. What is the best way to reduce the costs and at the same time to make the product more durable?

The best answer may be a greater emphasis on rulemaking. Whenever the living group mind yields a reasonably clear answer to a current problem, not only should the result be recorded, but a little more effort should be added so that the answer will be in the form of a rule that can always be available and useful, until such a time as the group mind sees fit to supersede it with a better rule.

PRECEDENTS

Until recently, the FGC seldom compared a current problem with a past decision. Without an index, files of comparable cases could not be found unless someone happened to remember them. Only very slight changes have been made. Decisions of the Mayor are sometimes available, and some cases in "The Collection" are available for use as precedents. The feeble efforts that have been made to use precedents as guides for exercising discretion can and should be strengthened. The aim should be not to record all decisions for use as precedents, but to select the decisions that might be most useful. The ones that deal with frequently recurring patterns of facts can be most useful, for they will most often come into play. Such decisions should be fully developed and published in *Avisen*. Of course, decisions made by the Mayor or the Director may be preferred to those made at lower levels. An index to the decisions should be kept up to date. Conceivably, a single index could be used for both rules and precedents.

In a normal development, the interaction between rules and precedents should be considerable. As questions are worked out through administrative precedents and policies become clarified, the disadvantageous spottiness of the system of precedents can be changed, so that whole areas of policy are clarified through rulemaking. Rules are especially helpful in rounding out the partial development of policies that comes from deciding particular cases.

Developing a system of precedents should be rather easy, because of what is already available. Applicants for aid are notified of denials by registered letters which state not only the decision but also reasons for it and the finding of facts. Favorable decisions appear as separate documents in the case folder.

American Comments on the Danish Family Guidance Center

In American eyes, the Danish accomplishment seems magnificent. The discretionary tailoring to the unique needs of each family is beautifully carried out. The discretion is startlingly broad: decisions are based on "highly individualized appraisals of economic, social, and psychological facts." The statute fixes no limit on the amounts of grants; it contains no provision governing the amounts. Mr. Busck amply supports his observations that the need of a family is appraised subjectively by the administrators and that the central element may be the personality, intellect, and feelings of the counselor, as well as the relationship that develops between the counselor and the family. Despite the breadth of all that discretion of the Family Guidance Center, the individual counselor exercises it without controlling rules, for Mr. Busck says that the instructions almost never answer questions that arise in individual cases.

The Family Guidance Center is surely inconsistent with the hypothesis that Europeans confine discretionary power more than Americans do. Americans do not trust their welfare administrators with such broad and unguided discretionary power. Even though discretion in America is much more confined, it is also much more abused. For instance, an excellent study of welfare administration in Virginia found that "systematic non-conformity with basic legal requirements goes uncorrected and apparently undetected" (J. L. Mashaw, Welfare Reform and Local Administration of Aid to Families with Dependent Children in Virginia, 57 Va. L. Rev. 818 [1971]). But Mr. Busck has searched for impropriety, bad judgment, or abuse of discretion in the Family Guidance Center, and he has found almost none.

The small organization of about one hundred, including fifty family counselors, seems tightly knit, efficient, and fair. Unlike their counterparts in Wisconsin, the individual workers are not overloaded; each counselor has about twenty cases at one time. The closest approach to an impropriety uncovered by Mr. Busck involves possibly excessive or unjustified payments, not refusals to pay those entitled to payments, although he does point out the lack of an effective check on negative findings of a family counselor.

The unusual reliance on staff meetings is an especially distinctive element in the system of control of discretion. The Director meets with senior officers once a month; he meets with all lawyers once each week; a supervisor meets with his counselors for an hour or more each week; and the seven lawyers meet for about an hour each week. The group work is an outstanding feature, and it seems to succeed in pulling toward equal justice.

Mr. Busck finds little to criticize, but he wants more recording of answers developed by "the living group mind" in the various meetings. Even so, despite my general belief in rulemaking as a device for cutting back excessive discretion and for guiding necessary discretion, Mr. Busck's account makes me wonder whether a good deal of group work can be about as effective as rulemaking—or possibly even more so. The group work produces good results, even though it is surely expensive.

Group work as a substitute for rule-making.

CHAPTER SIX

General Assistance in the Netherlands

A. A. M. F. STAATSEN

The General Assistance Act, which became effective in 1965, confers a right to public assistance upon everyone in the Netherlands. The rights under this statute are in addition to the rights to social insurance. Local governments administer the program, but 80 percent of the money comes from the central government.

The statute clarifies the formal framework of administration, but for the realities I have interviewed administrators of three municipalities, who stated to me both the facts and their opinions. After preparing a draft of this report, I discussed it with each office interviewed and made revisions.

Out of some 850 Dutch municipalities, I have chosen three for study—A, with a population of 170,000; B, with 80,000; and C, with 4,000. In C, I talked with the only caseworker, with a part-time helper, and with the mayor. In B, I interviewed four of the twenty-nine officers, including the Director of the Municipal Department of Welfare. In A, I was allowed to speak with only two officers out of thirty or more—a legal staff officer and the head of the subdepartment of general assistance, with whom I had four talks totaling about ten hours. I also interviewed two officers of the national government and a member of a committee of the Association of Directors of Welfare Departments. The committee is engaged in formulating rules concerning assistance administration by local governments. The fourteen first interviews and seven second interviews averaged about three hours in length.

THE STATUTORY FRAMEWORK

The statute does not explicitly grant discretionary power. It provides for financial assistance to one who does not have, or is in danger of not having, the means for the necessary cost of living. The statute provides that an individual has a right to public assistance when he needs it. The crucial word in the statutory term "necessary cost of living" is "necessary," and giving meaning to that term in individual cases involves discretion, especially since the statute provides that "the assistance has to be tuned to the circumstances and possibilities of the individual and his family." The explanatory memorandum states: "What an individual needs for his living depends very strongly on his personal circumstances. The question when and how much assistance has to be given, can only be answered on the basis of a judgment of the personal situation of the individual. The criterion is that of 'necessity.' . . . The determination is to a considerable extent a determination of policy."

Two main kinds of assistance are "normal" costs of living and "special" costs of living. The central government fixed a minimum in 1965 for normal costs of living (food, clothing, and housing) and fixed a maximum in 1971, in order to harmonize the policies of the 850 local governments; the amounts were fixed at about the level that two-thirds of recipients were then getting, and the other one-third were then getting more. Even though the 1971 statute specifies a maximum, the local government is still free to exceed the maximum "if this is necessary because of the personal circumstances of the individual." Such freedom involves a large discretionary power, as does the freedom to allow "special," as distinguished from "normal," costs of living. A "special" need includes such items as expense of a special diet, moving expenses, special household expense, tape recorders for the blind, or a car for one whose work or social contact requires it.

COMPETENCE AND ORGANIZATION

The power to administer public assistance is vested in the governing authority of each municipality, the Mayor and a number of city councillors. In A, which handles about 350 cases a week, the governing authority delegates to a director of the welfare department, who in turn delegates informally to his subordinates. In B, the director has delegated power to decide public assistance cases, but, in fact, he personally checks some of the sixty cases a week. In C, the governing authority itself deliberates about individual cases, sometimes even interviewing a claimant.

Municipality A operates with a good many unwritten rules, such as one that decisions of more than 1,500 guilders concerning a special need must be approved by the director, and decisions of more than 2,500 guilders must be approved by the governing authority.

In A the Welfare Department has three subdepartments, one of which administers the General Assistance Act. Under the head of the subdepartment are twenty-one caseworkers, three intake officers, three group leaders, and three deciding officers.

In B's system of administration the head of the subdepartment supervises twenty caseworkers, two intake officers, four group leaders, and three deciding officers.

One opinion expressed in C is that the single caseworker and his assistant should have their responsibility diffused, because a denial of a claim may produce threatening attitudes and personal insults from some citizens. Diffusion of responsibility could be accomplished through cooperation of several municipalities, so that no Welfare Department would have fewer than five officers.

None of the administrators has a university degree, except the director in A, but all have special education in the kind of welfare work they are doing.

PROCEDURE

The statute requires each city council to issue regulations to guide the handling of public assistance claims. The regulations are about the same in all three municipalities studied.

Although the statute allows a municipality to take the initiative, almost all cases are started by the claimant, who makes an oral or written request for assistance. The claimant gets a copy of the written application, which is prepared for him. An intake officer may exercise large discretionary power whenever he persuades an inquirer not to put in a claim, for the officer's view is unchecked. Perhaps a notice should be posted on the wall of each reception hall that any person has a right to put in a claim and to take an appeal.

In A, the caseworkers used to take turns as intake officers, but some of them avoided difficult problems by telling claimants to come back tomorrow, when another officer would face the difficulty. Now three intake officers serve permanently.

A caseworker usually visits the home of a claimant to investigate his personal and financial circumstances. In interviewing the claimant, he uses a list of questions, recording the answers on a form which the claimant signs. No copy of the form is given the claimant; probably it should be, because the claimant later may discuss the same questions with welfare officers, and because small print on the form obligates the claimant to inform the department about changes in his circumstances. The caseworker may check the information from the claimant, especially at the registry office and with the claimant's employer; this is usually done without the consent of the claimant.

Adverse decisions clearly should not be made on the basis of information which the claimant has no opportunity to explain or rebut, but it is not clear that the officers are governed by such a principle.

The caseworker makes a report of his findings and reasons. In B the report must be in the form appropriate for sending it to the claimant, but in A a report in that form is prepared by specialized people on the basis of the caseworker's report.

The group leader examines the report and sometimes requires further investigation. Any written exchange between the caseworker and group leader is withheld from the claimant, as it probably should be; the final report containing findings and reasons should suffice. What is important is that all facts that are adverse to the claimant should be stated so that the claimant may have full opportunity to rebut or explain them.

Otherwise, the claimant's right to ask for review by the governing authority is weakened or destroyed.

The case goes from the group leader to the deciding officer, who decides on the record. In B the deciding officer never has contact with a claimant, and in A he normally does not. The lack of such contact may mean that the deciding officer has a more objective view. Nearly all decisions of deciding officers are final, but an occasional case goes to the director or to the governing authority.

In A about 90 percent of decisions are explained by using one of the twenty standard formulas, some of which may be too vague. Saying that "you have not adequately established that assistance is necessary" is unfair to the claimant; he should be told specifically how the established facts are insufficient. Those who write the findings and reasons know that, the more they say, the greater the probability that they may be reversed; the less they say, the greater the probability that their decision will prevail with the appellate authorities. The system in B of assuring that the claimant always gets a full statement of reasons is superior to what is often done in A. In A and in C, however, a claimant can usually get an oral explanation from a caseworker by asking for it.

In C the procedure is very simple. The single caseworker reports to the governing authority, which asks questions, sometimes hears a claimant, and makes the determination.

LOCAL RULES AND RULEMAKING

Rules vary from one municipality to another. Officers of A use the *Handbook of General Assistance Administration,* prepared by the Association of Directors of Welfare Departments. In B the governing authority has formulated its own rules, and C's rules have been formulated in cooperation with some other municipalities. The differences seem explainable only by historical reasons, but the basic principles are usually about the same. The *Handbook* is about fifty-five pages long, but the rules used in C fill only twenty pages. An officer in C says the *Handbook* rules are too detailed.

Since the statute does not explicitly grant rulemaking power, the rules are considered informal and are merely guides. A 1971 statute authorizes rules which will "guide" the administration of general assistance "in order to achieve openness and clarity of assistance policy," but the exact legal force of the rules remains somewhat unclear. The explanatory memorandum regards the rules as "an administrative help." Most adjudication by the Crown (the highest reviewing authority under the General Assistance Act) concerns departures from the rules in order to administer individualized justice.

In practice, the rules are an instrument of major importance. For instance, one officer always has with him a copy of the local rules, even though he does not have the statutes. Any distinction between binding or formal rules and guiding or informal rules is generally too subtle for local administrators.

On the crucial subject of "normal" necessary cost of living, locating the precise point where rules end and discretion begins is difficult or impossible because the local administration can and must deviate from the rules in individual cases when necessary. For instance, rules in A and C provide that the amount of the payment must be adapted to the fact that a claimant has recently enjoyed a high income, so that during a transition period he may be given higher benefits than he would otherwise receive. The rules of B do not so provide, but the results are about the same. In B, the rules provide extra allowances for children in school, as compared with children not in school, but the rules of A and C contain no provision to that effect; even so, the results may be about the same. Rules answer some questions about "special" (as contrasted with "normal") costs of living. Some of them are more detailed in this regard than others. Consequently, the lines between "normal" and "special" costs of living are not clearly drawn.

One administrator may consider the purchase of a stove or a radio as "normal" and another may consider it "special," so the amount of the benefits may differ. The governing authority in one municipality may believe that the normal benefits are too low and may put pressure on administrators to be generous in allowing "special" benefits. Local administrators justify the inequality by saying that the national government is responsible for it by not specifying the budget of "normal" costs of living.

Even if a rule is clear in providing that a washing machine may be considered as a "special" expense, the question of whether it is necessary is often a discretionary one. Is it necessary for a single man? For a family with four children? For the aged and sick? The rules seem to leave a good deal for discretion, and the power to deviate from rules means much more discretion.

The price of a baby carriage varies from 100 to 600 guilders; how much should be allowed? When the answers are not clear, the decision is discretionary. In A, one officer makes a compilation of prices for common items twice a year; the compilation can be considered as an extension of the rules of the *Handbook* used in A.

For "special" expenses, the rules generally require that the claimant bear a proportion of the cost, but the proportion depends upon "payment capacity," which may be a variable. Some rules are definite: the "payment capacity" for visiting relatives in prison or hospital is 100 percent, and it is 20 percent for a blind man who needs a tape recorder. Yet deviation from such rules is permissible and common.

The dominant opinion in B is that rules are much needed. But officers in B make various statements, such as, "The entirety of rules must not become too extensive"; "It is impossible to formulate rules for problems that occur sporadically"; "The borderlines of policy change from day to day, and when rules are detailed they have to be often changed"; "Deviation from explicit and clear rules is difficult—it damages individualized justice"; or "There is no charm in applying detailed rules; officers then become robots."

The tendency in A is to make as few rules as possible, because "Officers shelter themselves behind rules, interpreting the rules strictly, and that damages individualized justice. Denials are too easy"; "Rules create inflexibility and impede evolution of opinion"; "Rules prevent consideration of all individual aspects of each case"; "The statute requires publication of rules.

We have strong objections to open rules. This is one reason we make as few rules as possible."

Even so, one can find within A much opinion in favor of written instructions on some subjects, and the head of the sub-department of general assistance has issued about thirty "operating instructions."

An officer in C says, "Nobody criticizes our assistance policy, so there is no need for rules. The main problems are covered by the present rules, and more extensive ones are not necessary."

Rules can be more extensive. They could properly answer whether or when telephone expenses are necessary, whether or when a refrigerator is necessary, whether a gas heater is necessary instead of a cheaper coal stove, or how much pocket money should be given to residents of a home for the aged.

The argument that no two cases are the same is hard to accept. Even in A, where some officers asserted this most emphatically, one person nevertheless estimated that 90 percent of all cases are decided according to a fixed pattern. Perhaps the rules can be quite detailed, but the officers should have full power to deviate when they strongly feel the need for individualizing. Caseworkers in B might be right in saying that rules are necessary "when we get too many complaints on a certain point," "when problems on a particular question too often occur," and "when a difference of opinion exists within the department." They object that a new baby carriage was allowed in one case and only a second-hand one in another identical case; they think a rule should prevent that kind of unequal treatment.

One danger is that rules will be followed even when the reasons for deviating from them are strong. Some personnel may find it easier to follow the rules in all cases, for that means doing the least thinking. But rules can be coupled with guides as to whether or when to deviate. Precedents about deviating can be as much a part of an officer's instructions as the rules from which he may deviate. Strict application of rules may be unjust when the reasons for deviation are especially strong. Unwritten practices or habits can be as much a part of the system as formal or informal rules; possibly the best results come from a shared sense of justice which is guided by rules. The right mixture of rules and discretion might sometimes be the optimum, except that in some areas the rules may be strong and clear and in other areas discretion may need to be dominant.

Of course, rules can be so detailed and complex that they cannot be administered by the kind of personnel who administer public assistance programs. Rules cannot be simple if they govern complex subject matter, but at some point the complexity becomes too much. A system of rules can break down when the complexity is more than an officer can be expected to administer. For that reason, problems involving many considerations usually must be solved through the use of discretionary power. But even when rules cannot govern complex subject matter, they can provide guides. A good rule can sometimes provide that the answer is in the discretion of the administrator, but it can go on and specify the particular factors that must be taken into account in exercising discretion. If the officer must evaluate, say, each of four factors that bear upon the ultimate question, and if he must state his evaluation of each, explaining why the four evaluations lead him to the conclusion he reaches, the needed discretion will be used—but, at the same time, the protection against arbitrary action will be considerable.

A rule can provide that an automatic washing machine is "necessary" for an unmarried mother with more than two children, except that it may be unnecessary if one child can help her do the washing, and it is not necessary if she lives with her parents who have a washing machine. Such a rule leaves a good deal to discretion—such as whether a teenage child in school who works after school can significantly help with the washing, whether use of a laundry in the neighborhood may be better, or whether the number of children younger than the one who can help is large enough to cancel out the effect of the help from that one child.

How long should an unmarried mother with a newborn child be entitled to assistance? At what point should she be required to have a job? What if the grandmother is able and willing to care for the child? What if the mother has several other children? Can rules and precedents answer most of the questions that arise? And how far can personnel be expected to interpret precedents when the controlling factors are multiple and of equal value?

The reaction of the officers to the idea that precedents can be useful is interesting. One reaction: "Too much work and we are already understaffed." But does a known precedent sometimes mean less work? Another reaction: "Too difficult, because a slight difference can justify an opposite result." But which is more difficult—to make a decision in light of a relevant precedent, or to make a decision without any precedent to use as a guide? For instance, consider the problem of how long an unmarried mother with a newborn child should be entitled to assistance if the grandmother will take care of the child. In a case in which the facts differ, is it easier or more difficult to decide if a precedent makes clear that the availability of the grandmother is a legally significant factor to take into account?

Everyone agrees that consistency from case to case is desirable, but opinions differ as to what means are helpful in achieving consistency. Using rules and precedents probably increases consistency, up to a point. Supervision of caseworkers by deciding officers in A, and by one deciding officer in B, as well as knowledge of and participation in each other's problems, probably encourages consistency. Caseworkers learn from decisions made in their own cases, and they also can learn from decisions made by other caseworkers. But the deciding officers can never take into account relevant facts that are not detected and reported by caseworkers, nor can they reverse an intake worker who wrongfully discourages an application. Effective communication is an absolute necessity if any organization is to achieve consistency in handling a multiplicity of questions. Leadership from top officers communicated all the way down the line, common training of workers, knowledge by workers of each other's attitudes and decisions, and shared philosophies all make for consistency.

Officers are sometimes "hawks" and "doves." Some think of public assistance as a privilege, regard claimants as too lazy to work, and consider an unmarried mother to be an unworthy sinner. But others deem the benefits too low and seize every opportunity to try to increase them. Any sizable staff may include both types. Differences among caseworkers are not always ironed out by deciding officers, for caseworkers may to a considerable extent control the decisions by emphasizing some facts and by failing to report others.

OPENNESS

The statute that authorizes rulemaking requires that the rules be made public, but no provision requires openness of decisions. The issuance of rules must be announced in one or more newspapers, and everyone may read them at the town hall. It should be possible to obtain a copy without charge or by paying the cost of printing.

The *Handbook of General Assistance* is published by a private publisher. Curiously, A violated the statute when it did not announce in the newspapers that it uses the rules of the *Handbook*. A published only the amounts of payments as to "normal" necessary costs of living. A copy of B's rules can be bought for only one guilder, and they were open to public inspection even before adoption of the statutory requirements. C's rules are published in cooperation with other municipalities using the same rules. Extensions of rules—such as lists of prices—are used as operating instructions but are not published. They should be published, or should at least be open to the public. Since precedents are nowhere used systematically, no such thing exists as open precedents.

The ordinary claimant, of course, is not likely to use the rules even when they are fully open and readily available. But representatives of labor unions and of organizations of welfare workers use the rules.

Officers in A are generally opposed to openness of any kind. Here are some opinions: "The public will not understand the rules"; "When rules are open, we have more work, because claimants not entitled to assistance have to be shown that the rules do not apply. Frustration results, because people come with hope and go away disappointed"; "Rules which are public prevent individualizing or make it more difficult. Deviating from published rules is not easy"; "Publishing rules creates a relation of 'attack and defense' between claimants and officers"; "Rules change too fast to make it feasible to publish them."

B's officers largely favor open rules, expressing such opinions as these: "Rules should be open. They are not easy to understand and are helpful to specialists who help people get assistance"; "One who reads the rules and wonders whether he is entitled to benefits comes to the office to ask for them. If he is wrong, the result can be explained to him."

In C, the officers did not see what purpose could be served by open rules. "If a claimant asks to see them, he can get them, but that is needless because he can get all the information he wants from the caseworkers."

The differing views should be overridden by the statutory obligation to publish rules. No public or private interests are harmed by the openness of rules, except that openness of rules may require effort to keep them up to date, and sometimes explanations must be made for departing from them.

Opening the files of decisions on individual cases would not be feasible because of the need for privacy. Yet if precedents were used more often, the files in larger cities might have a numerical system with names deleted, so that an outsider could compare decisions without invading anyone's privacy. But in this kind of administration, such a system would probably exalt systems of precedents too far.

CHECKING

Decisions of officers are sometimes reviewed by the director. One can ask that the governing authority review the director's decisions. A committee of the city council of A and of B advises in this regard.

When the higher authorities decide policy issues, their decisions have effect as precedents. Even so, the effects are usually small, because the unique features of particular cases are often emphasized. Decisions of the Crown guide assistance determinations only to a very limited extent.

Whenever a claimant is given more than he should be entitled to, the denial of equal justice to others who have similar cases is not corrected, for no one can make an appeal. The others who are denied what the one claimant gets are unlikely to know about the inequality.

Appeals are few. In A during 1970, 11,654 claims were decided, with about 4,200 denied, but only 180 of those sought review by the governing authority; twenty-one appealed to the Executive of the Province, and one to the Crown. Only twenty decisions were reversed.

The right of appeal is known, for a notice of the right accompanies the decision, and one who appeals need not be represented by counsel.

Checking is not limited to appeals, for subordinates are supervised at many points in administration. Heads of subdepartments, for instance, usually check each decision superficially before it becomes final. After all, caseworkers' recommendations are always passed upon by deciding officers. Since caseworkers usually learn of the decisions, in a sense the caseworkers check the decisions of the deciding officers.

A claimant who is dissatisfied with a caseworker may complain to a higher administrator. Group leaders often make their own investigations whenever they see fit to do so.

The director in A has consulting hours once a week, and he inquires into many cases. Sometimes so many people want to consult him that he needs help from as many as three of his assistants.

Opportunities for a dissatisfied claimant to get a new consideration of his case are abundant—perhaps even excessive. In addition to formal review, he can get informal reconsideration in many ways—perhaps in too many ways. He may go to that particular member of the governing authority who is responsible for welfare to try to obtain a favorable decision. (That member in A has consulting hours once a week.) He may even go to any member of the city council, who may then make his own inquiry of the administrators; it appears that the member of the council does not influence the result of the case, except to get it considered more quickly and perhaps more carefully. The many kinds of informal review produce a disorderliness and therefore a bit of inefficiency, but they may occasionally bring beneficial results and they probably do little harm.

CONCLUSION

Even though most officers interviewed emphasize individualized justice and therefore tend to oppose binding rules and binding precedents, the realities of administration are that the officers do develop more or less defined policies, so that in fact the rules and the established policies do largely control the results, without cutting off opportunity for individualizing. Probably many of the established principles and practices could be advantageously added to the formal regulations. Legislation proposed in 1971 would give the central government the power to formulate rules, thereby limiting the power of municipalities.

American Comments on Dutch General Assistance

What is most remarkable about Mr. Staatsen's study of Dutch welfare administration, in my opinion, is what he does not find. He does not find maladministration, vindictive administrators, disorganization, lawlessness of officers, or ignorance on the part of top-level bureaucrats. Yet I have done what I can to push him to find such items if they exist, and he has largely satisfied me that he has not found them because they are not there. If he is right in his firm finding—and we have no way of being absolutely sure—then probably Americans should be comparing Dutch successes with American failures in administration of welfare programs.

The American picture is far less beautiful than the Dutch picture Mr. Staatsen has painted. The outstanding American study may be Joel F. Handler and Ellen Jane Hollingsworth's *The "Deserving Poor"* (1971), which finds Wisconsin administration of aid to families of dependent children "intolerably

lawless," even though it may be one of the best state systems
in the United States. Whereas Mr. Staatsen describes administration which is firmly under the control of the managers and
in which discretion seems to be responsibly exercised and controlled, the Handler-Hollingsworth study emphasizes "the strat-
egy of withdrawal" of the caseworkers, caused by case overloads
and inclinations for "getting through the day as quickly and as
painlessly as possible, which means lack of individualized administration." The caseworkers are mostly young college gradu-
ates with only modest professional training who view their jobs
as way stations. Individualizing takes extra time and extra energy. The result: "For most clients there is no close supervision
of budget expenditures, no careful exploration of special needs
(unless the client raises the issue), no investigation of earned
income, no meaningful social service programs, and no real concern for moral behavior unless something happens to make the
case unusual" (p. 201). The authors even assert: "The bureaucracy is at present uncontrollable and therefore arbitrary and
unjust" (p. 205).

Mr. Staatsen makes some significant adverse criticisms of the
Dutch administration of general assistance, but instead of finding the system "intolerably lawless," he finds that "the rules and
the established policies do largely control the results, without
cutting off opportunity for individualizing." Nor does he find a
bureaucracy that is "uncontrollable" or "arbitrary and unjust."

If the Dutch do much better than Americans in administering a welfare program, why do they? What accounts for the difference? My best answer is that I do not know. But I think I do
know what the difference is not. It is not a difference in know-
how with respect to administration. The difference is in the
area of the will, rather than in the area of understanding how
to administer such a program. Americans are highly accomplished in administering somewhat comparable programs. For
instance, with all its faults, the Internal Revenue Service is in
an overall sense a magnificent success. So is the Social Security
Administration. Finding the reasons for the deficiency in the
American will to provide satisfactory administration of state
and local welfare programs might require a psychoanalysis of

the society, which I have no competence to make, but I surmise that the virtual absence of top administrators who firmly direct their staffs at all levels and who mold tightly disciplined organizations that effectively carry out the orders of the top administrators can be largely explained in terms of lack of incentives of the top administrators. A top administrator looks to the legislative body for guidance. And what he gets is ambivalence. The legislators are in turn responding to an ambivalent electorate. Does the electorate want a system of welfare administration that will effectively transfer public funds to all who are eligible to receive them, or does the electorate welcome the punitive attitude of welfare administrators that emphasizes the withholding of benefits from those who are regarded as undeserving?

Perhaps what I most admire about the general assistance administration in the Netherlands stems hardly at all from administrative know-how, and almost altogether from the relative firmness of the Dutch population and hence the Dutch Parliament in supporting an effective program of welfare administration.

Aside from the simple overall success of the program, Mr. Staatsen brings out a good many valuable details. I especially like his quotations from administrators about the idea of rulemaking, and his illustrations concerning the possible limits of rulemaking, openness, and use of precedents. His inquiries have no doubt stimulated some of the Dutch administrators to think further about those potentialities. Of course, the final answers to the questions about how far such devices will be useful have to come from experimentation. Perhaps the Netherlands will provide some of the leadership in doing the experimenting.

CHAPTER SEVEN

State Grants for the South of Italy

SABINO CASSESE

The Italian government makes grants to private corporations for a portion of the costs of constructing industrial plants in the South of Italy; the purpose of the program is to encourage faster economic development there. The grants differ from the more familiar credit incentives, which are loans, for the money granted is not to be paid back. For four years, the number and amounts of grants were: 1968, 1,588 grants, 69 billion lira; 1969, 1,534 grants, 60 billion lira; 1970, 846 grants, 63 billion lira; 1971, 1,424 grants, 66 billion lira.

The program began in 1950 mainly as a public works policy, but it was extended in 1957 to credit incentives, grants, and tax exemptions. Despite revisions of the statutes in 1965 and 1971, discussion continues in the newspapers and among academics on such questions as whether recipients of grants should be subject to special public controls, whether grants should be made to some enterprises in the North, and whether the proportion that goes to large corporations, as compared with medium and small corporations, is too high.

A study of discretion in administration of the grants seems desirable because Italian legal scholarship in administrative law has been focused in the Consiglio di Stato and on governmental action that restricts private rights, rather than on administrative practices or on governmental action conferring benefits. The Consiglio di Stato has decided four cases involving state grants for the South, but none of them relates to discretionary power. In 1967 the Consiglio di Stato, in its consultative and not its judicial function, stated that "the activity of the Ministry for the South consists in a simple assessment of the conformity of industrial enterprises to prescriptions and criteria of the 'piano di coordinamento.' On such technical questions, discretionary power is very limited, because the determination is based on criteria which fix strictly the category of enterprises and the amount of the grant." But Confindustria (an association of private industries) strongly opposed that view; it expressed the opinion that wide discretion was involved in the administration of state grants for the South, and it advocated that the system of grants be replaced by a system that would be automatic and simple, like credit incentives. Although the factual statements of the Consiglio di Stato and the Confindustria seem to reflect their respective ideologies, we shall see that discretion is found mainly in some cases where standards are lacking, and that such cases are not merely of minor interest. Recently Giovanni Russo observed (*Il Corriere della Sera*, November 29, 1973, p. 3) how confused the exercise of discretion was in the consideration of parts of big plants as separate units for the purpose of obtaining grants. Such criticisms did not come out sooner because of the administration's secrecy.

ORGANIZATION

The top agency is the interministerial committee for economic planning (C.I.P.E.), made up of ministers with powers in economic and social fields and headed by the Prime Minister. The predecessor of the C.I.P.E. was an ad hoc interministerial committee for the South. The work is done by the Cassa per il Mezzogiorno, an independent public corporation established in 1950, with a fund appropriated by Parliament. The President and the governing board of the Cassa are appointed by the council of ministers.

Inside the Cassa, grants are administered by the "servizio industria," a tripartite office which has about seventy employees. The administrative office receives applications, sends them to the instructing institute, prepares drafts of decisions, appoints the tester (together with the bureau for general affairs and contracts), and prepares payments to be made by the accounting office. The technical office gives advisory opinions requested by the other offices. The economic office makes studies and conducts research, especially on the economic impact of grants.

In addition, the Cassa has a planning bureau for coordination and research. Its role is mainly coordination among sectors, economic predictions, and distribution of funds among different sectors of the Cassa in carrying out decisions.

The original personnel of the Cassa were taken from the Ministry of Finance, the Ministry of Industry, and credit institutions.

THE STATUTES

The 1965 statute limited grants to 20 percent of expenses for buildings and equipment (*opere murarie, allacciamenti, macchinari e attrezzature*). A grant was based on a judgment of conformity by the Ministry of the South, according to the general criteria of the "coordination plan" approved by the interministerial committee for the South (later the C.I.P.E.). A "conformity judgment" is a determination that construction or a plan conforms to statutory requirements for a grant. The grant was made six months after completion of construction, on the basis of expenses incurred and inspections by the Cassa.

The 1971 statute authorizes grants of 35 percent for small enterprises with investments between 100 million and 1.5 billion, between 15 and 20 percent for medium-size enterprises with investments from 1.5 to 5 billion, and between 7 and 12 percent for large enterprises with investments of 5 billion or more. For small enterprises the amount is fixed by the statute, and the decision involves only the question of whether or not to make the grant; that decision is made on the basis of general criteria stated by a C.I.P.E. directive and a judgment of conformity given by the Ministry of the South.

The graduation of the grant for a medium-size enterprise is based on a decree of the Ministry in accordance with C.I.P.E. directives and the national economic plans. But no general rule governs the amount of a grant of between 7 and 12 percent for a large enterprise. The only guides are case-by-case decisions made by C.I.P.E. on the basis of promotion plans and general directives of C.I.P.E. itself, after an inquiry by the Ministry, in the framework of so-called programmed contracting, which is a procedure adopted in 1968 involving the collection of information in the first phase and meetings to discuss state action and private plans in the second phase. The model is the French "economic concerté."

Under the 1971 statute, the grant is no longer withheld until construction is completed, but is made in installments as the work progresses, with a final settlement three months after it is completed.

RULEMAKING

Four rules were issued under the 1965 statute—the "coordination plan" of 1966, a ministerial decree of 1967, and two ministerial decrees of 1969. The coordination plan was designed to decrease the percentage of the grant as the size of the recipient increases, and the decrees provided criteria about location, branch, and size, and about percentages based on size. Under the 1971 statute are the C.I.P.E. directives of 1972 and the ministerial decree of the same year. The directives deal only with criteria concerning location. The decree provides percentages for medium-size enterprises based on branch of activity and location.

In the Italian legal system, rules are made without party participation. Rules made by the C.I.P.E. are not made public, but the decree of the Ministry is published in the national official record. Although policy announcements are not specifically forbidden, they are not made, because of the trend toward the view that administrators must not do anything not explicitly authorized by statute; some even interpret the trend as an unwritten principle growing out of the principle of legality. The two reasons generally given for the absence of open rules and open policies are that the statute provides enough guidelines, and that industry and technology change too rapidly for a system of rules. Experience in making grants does not show such rapid change, and rules need not be as rigid as statutes. Rules could have been developed to guide determinations not guided by the statute, such as inclusion or exclusion of equipment that is not directly and stably connected with a building.

PROCEDURE

Applications are made by private entrepreneurs to the Cassa (for the grant) and to the Ministry of the South (or to a financial institute which passes it to the Ministry, for the conformity judgment). Under the old system, the first application was usually made at the end of construction, but under the new statute applications are made in advance. An application is in the nature of a response to a questionnaire.

A consultative body inside the Ministry (with representatives of the Cassa and of the Ministry of Industry) makes a decision assessing the conformity of the plans submitted to the criteria of the statute and the rules. The decision authorizes and directs the Cassa to pay, and it fixes the amount which can be paid as a percentage of the planned investment. The decision is not made public and is not given to the applicant but is sent to the financial institution and to the Cassa.

Simultaneously the financial institutions (medium or long-term bank: Isveimer, Irfis, Cis, Banca Nationale del Lovoro, Imi, Sezioni Speciali del Banco di Napoli e del Banco di Sicilia) prepare the instruction. If the application involves a grant only, the instructing banks will be the first three, which were set up with the participation of the Cassa. A very large number of applications pass through Isveimer. The instruction deals with credit incentives, because 95 to 97 percent of applicants ask for credit incentives as well as grants. Isveimer has twenty-two employees (five with technical training) and makes about six hundred reports a year. The main work is done by engineers and technicians, who are hired for each single examination. A scheme of questions is given to them, and an examiner discusses requests with the applicant. He evaluates the costs for buildings and the prices of equipment; his report is reviewed by Isveimer's technical officers, who rarely change any evaluation. No general written rules guide the examiner's work or its review, but sometimes meetings are held with examiners to discuss general changes in principles. The prevailing opinion at Isveimer is that each valuation is individualized, and that general rules are impossible. At the end, the bank sends a report to the Cassa, with maps, questionnaire, official records of the Chamber of Commerce, a list of equipment, and the time when construction is to be completed.

The second part of the instruction involves review of the report at an administrative level. The expenses are reexamined, and the percentage provided by the conformity judgment is translated into specific amounts of money. The only written guides deal with very limited subjects, such as transportation of frozen foods, issuing special checks, air and water pollution, and reduction of grants. For amounts over 100 million, the grant office may ask the technical office to compare prices with a general list of prices of the Ministry of Public Works. Then a monograph is prepared which is given to members of the board of the Cassa, the president, the director general, the account controllers, the accountancy, and the planning office.

Monographs become important precedents. A manual was prepared nine years ago on the basis of monographs stating findings and stating reasons for positive and negative decisions. This manual has been rapidly forgotten. Officers have changed, and recently even finding a copy of the manual has been difficult. The manual was prepared by Cassa employees without a directive of the council of administration, and it has not been kept abreast of the changes in the statutes, perhaps because of a lack of directive from senior officers or from the council of administration. But a monograph does sometimes quote from a precedent, and the common opinion is that precedents are very important; for this, officers give examples such as adequacy of stores at a plant, criteria to determine whether a plant is one unit or more than one, and the valuation of buildings for mixed uses (for instance, industrial and commercial). Instructions given internally for one case may become a "principle," yet precedents are used only inside the administration. No consideration is given to the idea of open precedents which will guide private parties. Cassa officers emphasize the practical difficulty of publishing all cases or of selecting leading cases. Secrecy of the precedents is the result.

The monograph is sent to the board of the Cassa, which makes the decision. A favorable decision is usually used by a private party to obtain loans from banks. If a monograph's conclusion is negative because the plant is outside the statute's provisions, the problem does not go to the board. Usually the board gives a brief motivation or statement of reasons, but findings and reasons are never given to interested parties. The applicant gets only the decision—the amount of the grant and the conditions. The Cassa officers say they have no reason to explain their findings. Reasons for decisions are stated in annual reports of the Cassa, but only in general figures and not for individual cases. Neither applicants nor other interested parties are allowed to know the basis for decisions.

After the Cassa's decision, the bank does some checking, private engineers make tests, and finally the accountancy office of the Cassa makes payments. If the Cassa learns of unlawful use of a grant (as for commercial instead of for industrial purposes), it may ask for restitution of unused portions. Appeals may be made to the Cassa within thirty days after a decision for correction of material errors, but in no case has departure from a precedent been urged as a basis for a finding of error. When an appeal is made to the Ministry, it sends the appeal to the Cassa. Only five appeals have been taken to the Consiglio di Stato during the past five years.

No hearings are held, and the informal conferences do not assure equal treatment. The large enterprises, which maintain specialized offices to deal with the Cassa, have greater access to the Cassa's officers and seem to have the advantage. One form of unequal treatment is earlier payments to large corporations and delayed payments to smaller ones. Administrators seem to regard the informal conferences as ways for them to get help in doing their work, not as ways of safeguarding the rights of applicants or of assuring equal treatment.

STANDARDS, POLICIES, AND ATTITUDES

The statutory guides are so elastic that underlying policies are somewhat responsive to political pressures. The Confindustria advocates the concentration of grants in some limited zones and in large enterprises, with an automatic and mechanical administration of grants. The Consiglio di Stato, which usually deals with state action restricting private enterprise and seldom deals with governmental largess, deemphasizes the problem of discretion, apparently unaware of the breadth of discretion that is required. On the much-discussed issue of favoring large enterprise, the statutory movement has been from the 1957 limitation of grants to enterprises with less than 1.5 billion investment to the 1959 ceiling of 3 billion and the 1961 ceiling of 6 billion.

Statutes allowing grants for buildings and equipment are unclear about some items, such as auto-cement-mixers, railway coaches, or pipelines out of a plant; these problems have been solved on a case-by-case basis, without guiding standards. Administrators claim that advance codification is impossible because of technological advances. A special problem has been whether or when a number of small plants should be counted as one unit, since the percentage may be higher for a smaller unit. Remarks were made in Parliament that subdivision of an investment into many small plants is against the law, but the Ministry allowed such subdivision, without guiding standards. Guidelines have been lacking for evaluating portions of plants used for both commercial and industrial purposes. It seems strange that the Cassa has never tried to use decisions in new cases as guides for solving the new problems. For instance, a rule could provide that grants can be made for equipment if 70 percent of that equipment's capacity is used for needs of the plant.

OPENNESS AND SECRECY

Although many scholars fear the preeminence of administration due to its weight, size, and authoritative powers, such is not the Italian situation. Administration is institutionally weak;

it is often dominated by the strength of private interests, and demands a defense against the pressures of such interests. From such background the necessity of secrecy seems to grow—to avoid open and fixed standards and rules, which would weaken administrative action and make it too rigid, as compared with private flexibility. But such an administrative response pushes toward an authoritarian and closed system that fails to distinguish interests of small enterprises from dangerous and powerful interests.

Openness needs to be considered in more detail. First, figures are unavailable as to how much money flows through state contributions to big, medium, and small companies, but the widespread impression is that most of it goes to large companies. No reports are made to Parliament or to the public that contain figures about the amount of grants that go to large, medium, and small corporations, and no such reports are made as to how much goes to each named corporation. Second, there is no countervailing power; most of the big companies are publicly owned (with members of boards appointed by the government) and in a better position to "discuss" with the Cassa than private enterprises. Third, organizations do not exist to defend general, widespread interests, such as those of taxpayers.

Secrecy and impersonality serve less as instruments to protect a weak administration from assaults of strong interests than as means of avoiding public controls on the use of public money. Secrecy as a rule of procedure in the administration comes also from prevalent Italian legal education—from a widespread attitude which favors routine instead of innovation. The tradition is secrecy, and openness requires innovation.

Decisions are now given to applicants, but without reasons. The main question about openness is whether reasoned decisions could be available to others. It has been said regarding the United States that what the future has in store is a combination of judicial requirement of administrative clarification of standards to guide discretion with a judicial requirement of findings and reasons that relate the standards to the facts of the particular case. This statement can perhaps be considered valid in Italy for cases that are frequently reviewed by the Consiglio di Stato, but government largess for the development of the

South is not often reviewed. Government largess is intended not to enrich private individuals, but to reach social goals. The primary interest to be protected is that of the public, not that of the applicants.

One possibility would be to open to the public the leading decisions and the reasons for them. Another possibility is to open to the public all decisions and all reasons. Opening leading cases would be useful only if they became authoritative precedents, but the present practice is for administration to avoid being bound by precedents. Opening all cases to public inspection may therefore be better. Taxpayers should be entitled to know the amounts paid to large, medium, and small companies, and the amounts for each province and for each economic sector. The main reason administrators give for resisting openness is the need for protecting patents, but patents can be protected while opening most other information.

Even though applicants, especially large ones, have easy access to administrators, and even though administrators are subjected to no influences in the opposite direction, the secrecy excludes public opinion as a control on discretion. Neither in parliamentary debates nor in newspapers does one find a discussion of the Cassa's exercise of discretion.

American Comments on Italian Subsidies

The paper by Professor Cassese has a good deal more significance than a hurried reader of it is likely to discern. Even though the amounts of money are large, the discretion is broad and is little controlled. Indeed, the discretion might be the broadest and least controlled of all the discretion discussed in this symposium.

Athough the discretion involved in "conformity judgments" (deciding whether a construction plan fits statutory requirements) is usually narrow, the percentage of construction costs that will be granted is 7 to 12 percent for large corporations and 15 to 20 percent for medium corporations, and Professor

Cassese says flatly that no general rule governs the amount of the grant. Furthermore, even though a manual was prepared stating reasons for positive and negative decisions, he says that "the manual has been rapidly forgotten," and that "the statutory guides are so elastic that underlying policies are in some measure responsive to political pressures." He finds "a deliberate purpose to avoid open and fixed standards and rules" and a push toward "an authoritarian and closed system."

One with a background in American administrative law would expect that in such a program general rules would rapidly develop that would govern results or would at least guide discretion. One would also expect that the manner of application of such rules would gradually be controlled by open precedents. The rules would generally be made through rulemaking procedure—giving affected parties notice and invitations to send in written comments, submit data, state preferences, and try to persuade. But in the Italian program of grants for the South, rules are of little consequence, and such rules as are made are made "without party participation." Rules do not grow up through the case law, for Professor Cassese says that new cases are not used as guides, even though, for instance, a rule could provide that grants can be made for equipment if 70 percent of that equipment's capacity is used for needs of the plant.

Each of three items seems to American eyes to be unfortunate, but the three in combination seem even shocking. First, applicants are not given reasons when their applications are denied or when the amounts are less than expected. Second, standards, rules, and precedents to guide or govern discretion are almost completely lacking. And, finally, on that background the administrators maintain secrecy about the recipients of grants and about the amounts. Neither Parliament nor the public is allowed to know who gets how much!

Surely inquiries of the kind that Professor Cassese has made can be profitable to all concerned—except those who may be unduly benefited by the system. Should not Members of Parliament keep the administrators in check? Should not taxpayers have a chance to know who gets their money, how much, and why? Should not professors in universities inform themselves of the realities of such a system of administration? Should not students of administrative law, instead of being limited to learning about the Consiglio di Stato, be introduced to the administrative decisions that matter, who makes them, how they are made, on what basis, and under whose influence?

CHAPTER EIGHT

Tax Relief Contracts in France

CHRISTIAN MERLIN

One way the French government induces private business to carry out policies formulated by the government is by purchasing compliance through tax relief contracts. In consideration for a corporation's compliance in specified degrees and ways, the government agrees to relieve the corporation of a specified percentage of its taxes for a specified period, or a specified portion of particular taxes. The theory is that free enterprise is left free, but the businessman is given an economic incentive to go along with the government's policy.

For instance, one major governmental policy is to encourage decentralization from the congested Paris region. Moving a plant from the Paris region to some other part of France may be expensive and may involve other disadvantages. But if the tax inducement is large enough, a decision, based exclusively on business advantages and disadvantages, may be made to move the plant. No command is issued. No one is coerced. But the government's policies are carried out. The decision as to how much tax relief should be awarded in any particular case is highly individualized. Yet litigation about the program, that is, review by the administrative court, is almost nonexistent. Cases involving tax relief contracts have rarely gone to the Conseil d'Etat.

France has had a series of Economic and Social Development Plans with which the tax relief contracts have been linked, although some such contracts began as early as 1938, predating the First Plan (1947–53). The types of tax relief contracts have grown gradually—fifteen were available during the Fourth

Plan (1962–65), and thirty during the Fifth Plan (1966–70). Yet, because of a crisis in the French planning system, no new type of contract has developed since 1968.

The vast multiplication of tax relief contracts is evidence of their success, but the system does not always provide full satisfaction. Critics charge discrimination among taxpayers in violation of the principle of equal protection. Parliament has authorized each type of contract, but the charges are directed to administrative action, not to legislative action. The Ministry of Finance has enormous discretionary power, which it exercises with a seeming obsession for secrecy, and accusations of discriminatory decisions are hardly surprising.

French tax statutes are like American ones in providing for deductions and exemptions for classes of taxpayers, but the statutes have no American counterparts in their provisions for tax relief contracts. Unlike ordinary deductions and exemptions which are governed by law that is applied equally to members of each class of taxpayers, the determination of who gets a tax relief contract and in what amount depends not simply upon application of law to the facts of each case but upon individualized determinations by the Ministry of Finance that are highly discretionary and that are often mostly unguided either by statutes or by administrative rules.

Tax relief is regarded as a privilege, because it is in contravention of the common fiscal law that is normally applicable, and because under the statutes no one has a legal right to such tax relief. Tax relief is not automatically awarded on the basis of entitlement under the statute and under the rules, because no one is entitled to it. Decisions awarding tax relief are always individualized, tailored to the immediate unique circumstances of each particular taxpayer. That is why the decisions have to be discretionary.

The statutes, which are numerous and which have been enacted over a period of more than thirty years, have all been drafted along similar lines. No such statute is deeply dissimilar to the others. The statutes contain hardly any criteria to guide the award of tax relief contracts. An example is Article 26 of a statute of 31-7-62: "Corporations which have premises built for their industrial and commercial use may be authorized by a tax relief contract granted by the Ministry of Finance, after consultation with a committee of the Fonds de Developpement Economique et Social (FDES) to apply for an exceptional redemption of 25% of the cost price." Another example is Article 27 of the same statute: "Subject to a preliminary tax relief contract, granted by the Ministry of Finance, after consultation with a committee of FDES, and in the proportion defined by the tax relief contract, corporations which merge may carry forward previous deficits not previously deducted, on the future profits of the merged corporations."

Two other statutory provisions should be mentioned. One is Article 38 of a statute of 12-7-65: "Tax relief contracts are granted by the Minister of Finance. Administrative rules of the Ministry may set up simplified procedures, and may delegate the decision-making power to civil servants of the tax administration having at least the rank of Directeur Departemental." Article 17 of a statute of 26-12-69 provides: "Administrative rules by the Ministry of Finance, issued after consultation with a committee of FDES, may define, taking into account the importance, the nature, or the location of the considered activities, the conditions for granting tax relief contracts to which fiscal exonerations are attached, according to existing statutes or regulations."

Those who draft laws for the French Parliament (always inspired, in this area, by the Minister of Finance) impose no important limits on the powers of the Minister, and the resulting vagueness leaves him with unconfined and unguided discretionary power to define the conditions for the award of tax relief contracts.

To understand the role of administrative rules in confining the discretion of the Ministry, let us consider an example. A 1953 statute provides for tax relief contracts for industrial or commercial corporations moving from heavily industrialized regions (especially Paris) with respect to ownership transfer taxes and taxes on real estate acquisitions, but the conditions were left to the discretion of the Ministry of Finance. The Minister issued a *décret* establishing that a tax relief contract may be granted in case of "creation or extension of an industrial or commercial corporation in regions where, considering the demographic evolution and the economic development level, an imbalance between labor supply and demand appears or can appear." Under such a vague rule, no corporation can know whether or not it is eligible for a tax relief contract. To enforce the *décret* the Ministry published an instruction during 1964, explaining to civil servants how to decide individual cases. But even the instruction gives no precise detail as to how to apply the vague criteria; instead, the instruction merely sets forth the procedure. Civil servants who were interviewed acknowledge that they do apply more precise criteria than those contained in the rule or in the instruction, but the criteria used are unpublished and are unknown to the corporations affected. Despite some consistency of criteria from one case to another, a corporation which satisfies all requirements still *is not entitled* to a tax relief contract. The requirement that a corporation comply with unknown criteria means that the Ministry's discretion is limited only by such limits as it imposes on itself in any individual case.

Except for a 1938 experiment with tax relief contracts, all of the thirty types of such contracts have been created since 1948, and their creation is spread rather evenly over the period from 1948 to 1968. They apply to nearly all fields of economic life: creation of corporations, concentration, location, exports, research. Some of the policies are: concentration of foreign French business and promotion of research in foreign markets (thirteen types of tax relief contracts); geographical planning (six types); scientific and technical research, including the financing of intellectual investments (three types); underdeveloped parts of French overseas territories (eight types).

Administrative procedures in awarding tax relief contracts were developed through administrative practice. The first statutory guidance for such procedures did not come until 1965. The types of tax relief contracts have been normally proposed by specialized commissions in charge of preparation of each Plan and have been generally provided for by the Plan. But the Ministry of Finance has drafted each statute and each implementation measure. The most important judgment—whether the cost in tax money is commensurate with the expected benefits—depends almost entirely on the Minister's discretion. Of course, the content of each Plan guides the particular determinations; each new Plan changes the guides. But the Plan and the statute are typically so vague ("the general economic interest"; "the normal action of competition"; "the improvement of the structure of corporations") that rules adopted under one Plan often need not be changed to reflect a new Plan, and when a statute assigns a competence, it may fail to state goals but may grant power to the administration to determine goals. When the administration enforces rules strictly against one taxpayer and exempts others, the Conseil d'Etat merely says that "the terms of the statute have neither as a goal nor as an effect to compel the administration to grant or deny a tax relief contract" (Ville du Perray en Yvelines, Conseil d'Etat, November 29, 1968).

The Ministry of Finance publishes in the official journal or bulletin the conditions a corporation must comply with to qualify for a particular type of tax relief. Such conditions are formulated on recommendation of the Fonds de Developpement Economique et Social (FDES), composed of civil servants of the Ministry of Finance and other ministries.

A corporation applies for a contract by answering a questionnaire. A special committee of the FDES then makes a recommendation, sometimes after negotiating with the corporation. The decision is usually made for the Minister of Finance by the Directeur General des Impots (Director of the Tax System).

The contract provides for the designated tax relief, subject to whole or partial withdrawal and subject to a discretionary monetary penalty if the corporation fails to fulfill its agreed undertaking. The contract states, of course, the program the corporation agrees to carry out, the conditions, and the time limits.

Recently, in view of multiplication and diversity of tax relief contracts, an effort has been made toward unification, deconcentration, and selection. The questionnaire has been standardized, and substantive conditions to the grant of tax relief have been unified. Powers have been delegated to Regional Tax Directors (Directeurs Regionaux des Impots), who now handle about 75 percent of applications, subject to appeal to the Minister and to handling by the Minister if the amounts exceed designated figures. Some little-used types of contracts were discontinued in 1965. That the award of some contracts has become quasi-automatic does not change the fact that the important contracts are negotiated without publicity or safeguards.

Until recently large corporations with their staffs of accountants and lawyers had an important advantage in the face of the variety of contracts, the multiplicity of formalities, and the shortage of information. But the advantage is diminishing as small corporations are calling on legal counselors' advice. Since decisions are not published, no corporation knows which of its competitors have been awarded a contract or on what terms. Review by the Conseil d'Etat is not a protection, since its nullification of a refusal of an award never amounts to an award; the Conseil may require reasons for a refusal, but it cannot inquire into the merits.

The broad discretion, combined with secrecy, gives rise to the question whether large corporations are the main beneficiaries. Control by Parliament is limited by lack of information on the part of individual M.P.'s, and published data do not enable Parliament to exercise significant control. Policies known to the staff of the Ministry are concealed from applicants. Of two applications that seem the same, one may be granted and one denied, with no stated reason. Oral explanations are sometimes made, but civil servants in the Ministry are strictly forbidden to give written explanations. Neither arbitration nor adversary procedure is ever available. The Minister's power to individualize seems to be a nearly absolute power.

Information about tax relief contracts published in the *Bulletin* of the Minister of Finance is limited to the number of applications granted each year, their regional distribution, and the global turnover of each type of contract. No information is given about the corporations themselves, even without identifying them. Yet, according to unofficial staff estimates, for an investment of ten million francs, including two million for land and eight million for buildings and equipment, a corporation which decentralizes a factory in the Paris region can save up to one million through a tax relief contract, in addition to a special provision for depreciation of two million. Other government sources (essentially through FDES) may provide subsidies of 6 to 25 percent of the investment.

Large corporations are the main beneficiaries for several reasons. Such program objectives as those relating to concentration, scientific research, and decentralization are often inapplicable to small companies. For instance, a minimum requirement for decentralization contracts is an investment of 300,000 francs and the creation of thirty jobs, even though only 1.5 percent of French corporations employ fifty workers or more; 706,421 corporations out of 729,125 employ fewer than fifty workers. In 1959 the administration made a timid effort to help small and average-sized corporations by creating a type of tax relief contract for companies with less than 500 workers and capital of five million francs or less. A group of small corporations may create a common corporation at a regional level for such important services as purchasing, improving product quality, or exporting, and the common corporation may be eligible for tax relief contracts. But French businessmen who manage small corporations are very unwilling to group together.

The number of tax relief contracts was about 5,000 in 1965 (2,000 for decentralization and 500 for concentrating and restructuring corporations), and about 10,000 in 1968. Many large corporations benefit from multiple contracts at any one time, so only a privileged minority is concerned. Only the large corporations have the requisite information, techniques, specialized advisers, and contacts with high-level civil servants.

We turn now to two questions: What is the degree of discretionary injustice, and what remedies are feasible?

In the case of Société Maison Genestal, decided by the Conseil d'Etat 26-1-68, the Minister of Finance had stated that the applicant's plan "did not seem to involve, at the general in-

terest level, sufficient economic interests and advantages to
justify the grant of a tax relief contract to which is attached a
substantial tax exemption." The Conseil found this statement
too vague for it to review the legality of the decision and required a more specific statement of reasons. It is now a
recognized principle that the Conseil may require administrators to state to the Conseil the reasons for decisions, even when
the statute does not so require. But in a case that does not go
to the Conseil, the administrators are not required to state
reasons to the applicant. The control resulting from a requirement of reasons stated to the Conseil does not involve a careful examination of the facts of the case.

The Ministry in most cases enforces some previously defined
criteria, yet the Conseil d'Etat forbids the Ministry to bind its
own discretion in advance by rules or standards. The Ministry
thus seems to be doing precisely what the Conseil forbids.

When the Conseil requires the Ministry to explain reasons
for a decision, the Ministry is in the dilemma of stating the
policy it has added to the conditions of the statute, thus
violating the Conseil's prohibition laid down in the Brabant
case, or stating fictitious reasons that did not in fact motivate
the decision. The decision of the Conseil thus contributes to
the tendency toward administrative secrecy. One effective
policy that the Ministry tends to keep secret is that a larger
corporation is favored over a smaller corporation.

An outstanding example that comes out in interviews with
civil servants is that of a large industrial corporation which had
some of its factories in Paris. The administration wanted to use
the land of one factory as part of its town planning policy, and
the corporation agreed to move outside the city of Paris but
still inside the region of Paris. For the move it was given a tax
relief contract, even though the statute authorized such a contract only for a move outside the region of Paris. The basic
decentralization policy was furthered in a way that the statute
did not authorize. The size of the corporation and of its factory
was the decisive factor, for no tax relief contracts have been
granted in such circumstances to smaller corporations.

In another example, two corporations applied for tax relief

contracts for establishing new industrial plants outside the Paris region. Although they did not manufacture the same products, they had similar structures and turnover. One was granted a contract and the other was denied it. The decisive factor was that the one was larger than the other, creating more jobs. We shall not discuss the question whether the policy was desirable, but the statute does not authorize the policy of favoring the larger corporation.

Since only 1.5 percent of French corporations employ fifty workers or more, a policy of denying tax relief contracts to corporations with less than fifty workers means that 98.5 percent of corporations are in fact ineligible for such contracts. The policy adds essential conditions to the statute and introduces rules which bind the administration. No control seems possible over such informal policy.

The Conseil d'Etat in a recent decision, Crédit Foncier de France, 11-12-70, has recognized that the Minister of Finance has authority to make guidelines in the field of tax relief contracts. The authority is linked to the prohibition against discrimination in the exercise of discretionary power. Objective criteria are required in administering the economic incentives, and it is important that these criteria be known by all who are interested. But the Conseil has decided that exceptions to rules or guidelines should always be possible in order to cope with unexpected situations.

Information about tax relief contracts should be available to the public, including the rules and guidelines for granting and denying such contracts, the cost to the government of each type of contract, the benefits to the government and to the public of each type of contract, and the detailed facts about each corporation which has such a contract. Such information should assist in maintaining parliamentary control. A consultative committee, composed of staff members of the Ministry of Finance and an equal number of representatives of taxpayers, should arbitrate all disputed cases before any case goes to an administrative court.

The main problem, however, lies in the reinforcement of legality in the economic field. Statutes are imprecise, and the complexity and movement of economic situations require administrative discretion. The legality must not be a hindrance, or it will not fulfill its function, which is to give the administration the powers it needs but at the same time to put conditions on its exercise. The major difficulty in the economic field is to find new formulations for these legal conditions.

A fundamental improvement would be acknowledgment by the Conseil d'Etat of the need for the Ministry of Finance to make binding rules. The Ministry should be allowed to limit its own powers by published rules, without special legislative authorization, stating the conditions and the criteria used in the selection of applicants. Only the administration, which has a complete knowledge of the economic evolution resulting from applications, is able to formulate the criteria and adapt them to shifting problems, in conformity with the statutory objectives.

A rulemaking power is needed for tax relief contracts, separate from the general rulemaking power of the government. When the Ministry is confronted with a problem not governed by any published criterion, a solution might be borrowed from the German law, which gives a specific place to the administrative custom among the sources of the law; the administration is bound by the previously adopted attitude in similar cases and must either hold to it or explicitly state specific reasons for departing from it. Such a system would reinforce the principle of legality, for rules would grow out of the usual attitude of the administration.

American Comments on French Tax Relief Contracts

The discretionary power of the French Ministry of Finance in awarding and denying tax relief contracts and in determining their amounts seems enormous; yet it is little confined, mostly unguided by rules or standards, and almost never checked by

have made the desirable correction. In Merchandise Transport Ltd. v. British Transport Commission, [1962] Q.B. 173, Danckwerts, L.J., said: "If the tribunal makes a practice of relying on previous decisions in respect of other applications . . . there is, in my opinion, danger that the discretion of the tribunal may not be applied in an unfettered and proper manner having regard to the merits of the particular case." That holding and others supported the statement of a careful writer that "a tribunal entrusted with a discretion must not, by the adoption of a general rule of policy, disable itself from exercising its discretion in individual cases." De Smith, Judicial Review of Administrative Action 294 (2d ed. 1968). But that position was changed by the House of Lords in British Oxygen Co. Ltd. v. Minister of Technology, [1970] 3 W.L.R. 488. A statute provided that the Board of Trade "may make to any person carrying on a business in Great Britain a grant towards approved capital expenditure incurred by that person in providing new machinery or plant for use in Great Britain." The Board adopted a rule to deny grants for any item of plant costing less than £25. Lord Reid asserted that "if the Minister thinks that policy or good administration requires the operation of some limiting rule, I find nothing to stop him." Viscount Dilhorn said that "it was both reasonable and right that the Board should make known to those interested the policy it was going to follow." In a later case, the court said that "it is perfectly legitimate for an administrative body such as this . . . to lay down a general policy which it proposes to adopt in the cases coming before it" (Cumings v. Birkenhead Corp., [1971] 2 All E.R. 881).

That both the French and the British reviewing authorities have had to move away from their own precedents in order to establish the sound position that administrators may limit their own discretion by rules, standards, or guides seems to show the subtlety of the problem but also shows that discerning judges can surmount the problem. American authorities have been somewhat inconsistent, too, but probably American courts will follow the outstanding opinion of Judge Friendly in Fook Hong Mak v. Immigration and Naturalization Service, 435

F.2d 728 (2d Cir. 1970): "We are unable to understand why there should be any general principle forbidding an administrator, vested with discretionary power, to determine by appropriate rulemaking that he will not use it in favor of a particular class on a case-by-case basis, if his determination is founded in considerations rationally related to the statute he is administering."

What probably actuated both the French and the British courts in their initial decisions was the thoroughly sound idea that a rule should not be allowed to cut into needed individualizing. Administrators who want to avoid the extra work of individualizing sometimes adopt a simple rule that easily takes care of whole batches of cases, and reviewing authorities sense that the results need to be tailored to the unique facts and circumstances of each case. The need for individualizing should be protected, but at the same time, precedents which are properly individualized should be followed unless they are overruled. Rules, standards, and guides should cut back discretion to the point where individualizing is needed.

6. Should the next step for the Conseil d'Etat in receding from the Brabant position be not merely to *allow* rules or guidelines, but to *require* them, as far as feasible?

Every advanced legal system in the world relies on rules and principles in order that courts will not have unfettered discretion in administering justice; for the same reason, rules and principles are desirable when administrators instead of courts are making the decisions. Discretion is needed by both courts and administrators, but discretion should not go beyond what is needed. Yet it generally does, because legislative bodies usually do not know how to cut it back to what is needed. Administrators usually do know how, on each particular subject within their specialized areas. Therefore, in my opinion, the reviewing authorities should *require* administrators, as far as feasible, to formulate rules, instructions, standards, or guidelines to govern or to guide the administrators in deciding questions that have been legislatively committed to their discretion. But such discretion as is necessary for needed individualizing in particular cases should be preserved.

What I have just said is in line with what the Conseil d'Etat said in the Crédit Foncier case, except that I would have the Conseil require what it now allows.

The idea of requiring administrative rulemaking in order to eliminate *unnecessary* discretionary power, while preserving and protecting the discretionary power that is needed in order to provide the desirable individualizing, is in the ascendancy in American law. I have a collection of about three dozen cases in which American courts have adopted the idea. I shall discuss two of them.

One of the simplest cases is Holmes v. New York City Housing Authority, 398 F.2d 272 (2d Cir. 1968). The Authority had about 90,000 applications for houses each year but only about 10,000 houses. No statutory standard guided the selections, and the Authority itself developed no standard. The court held that "due process requires that selections among applicants be made in accordance with 'ascertainable standards.'" Another way of stating the holding is by saying that the agency must cut back its unfettered discretion so that it will not be unguided by standards. But the discretion needed for individualizing will remain.

Another outstanding case is Environmental Defense Fund v. Ruckelshaus, 439 F.2d 584 (D.C. Cir. 1971). In reviewing an administrative refusal to suspend the registration of DDT, the court declared that the administrator "has an obligation to articulate the criteria that he develops in making each individual decision." The court went on to make a rather dramatic statement:

> We stand on the threshold of a new era in the history of the long and fruitful collaboration of administrative agencies and reviewing courts. . . . Judicial review must operate to ensure that the administrative process itself will confine and control the exercise of discretion. . . . When administrators provide a framework for principled decision making, the result will be to diminish the importance of judicial review by enhancing the integrity of the administrative process, and to improve the quality of judicial review in those cases where judicial review is sought.

The Supreme Court of the United States has not yet rendered a clean-cut decision in support of the lower courts' requirement of administrative rulemaking to cut back unnecessary discretion, but a prediction that it is likely to do so at an early time can be confidently made. A close approach was Morton v. Ruiz, 415 U.S. 199 (1974). Although the holding was intertwined with other complex issues from which it cannot be separated, the Court's language and attitude are significant to our present context. The Court said that in determining what Indians are eligible for welfare benefits, the Bureau of Indian Affairs "must, at a minimum, let the standard be generally known so as to assure that it is being applied consistently and so as to avoid both the reality and the appearance of arbitrary denial of benefits to potential beneficiaries." The idea that the Bureau must "let the standard be generally known" is precisely the thought that I am emphasizing. The Court also said, in what I think may be an overstatement: "No matter how rational or consistent with congressional intent a particular decision might be, the determination of eligibility cannot be made on an *ad hoc* basis by the dispenser of the funds." The Court's push against *ad hoc* decisions is needed, but the whole push will fail if it attempts more than can reasonably be achieved. *Ad hoc* decisions cannot be eliminated; the Court itself makes such decisions, because it has to. The goal should not be elimination of *ad hoc* decisions; it should be principled decisions as far as feasible, supported by reasoned opinions when feasible, but with room for *ad hoc* decisions to whatever extent individualizing is needed. Even so, what the Court asserted in the Ruiz opinion pulls in the right direction, even though some tempering of the statement may become necessary.

My main reaction to the Merlin paper is that the French legal profession, including especially those concerned with legal education, should give attention to problems of justice or injustice in the administrative process, whether or not those problems come to the Conseil d'Etat. My half-dozen questions about the Conseil are of only secondary importance.

CHAPTER NINE

Administration of the Dutch Policy for Option-Regretters

J. A. J. SCHEFFERS, A. B. RINGELING, AND R. P. WOLTERS

When Indonesia became independent of the Netherlands in 1949, the residents of Indonesia who were of Indonesian descent naturally took on Indonesian nationality, while those of Dutch or other European descent retained their Dutch or other European nationality. But people of mixed descent, mostly the offspring of Dutch men and Indonesian women, were given a chance to choose either of the two nationalities. Many chose Indonesian nationality, and then later regretted their choice. We are calling such people "option-regretters." They are the subject of this paper.

At the time of the option in 1950 and 1951, some people had high expectations for quick economic revival of Indonesia. Employers preferred Indonesians to Dutch, the new constitution guaranteed certain rights to all Indonesians, and both the Union of Indo-Europeans and the Dutch High Commissioner in Indonesia recommended Indonesian nationality. Other people worried about the unstable and worsening Indonesian political situation, the collapse of federalism and its replacement by a unitarian republic, decline of the economic condition, educa-

The study is based on examination of the files, especially dossiers of individual cases, and on interviews with the officials having something to do with making the policy.

We are grateful to Professor Davis for his advice and for making this study possible, to all the people who were interviewed for their extra work on overloaded days, to Mr. Van Aartsen of the Justice Department and his staff for their unfailing help, to all those who criticized earlier drafts, and to Miss Van den Berg and Miss Huysmans for patiently typing scores of drafts.

tional advancement (because Dutch was banned as a language in the public schools), threats of nationalists, and condemnation of Indonesian nationality by, among others, a pressure group for "Greater Netherlands." [1]

Of about 200,000 Indo-Europeans, 13,666 options were made for Indonesian nationality, involving approximately 31,000 people. Nearly half of the options were made in the last month of the period, most of these after the recommendation of the Dutch High Commissioner. During the period 1951–57 many were regretting their option for Indonesian nationality, and the Dutch government began to realize that many applications would be made for admission to the Netherlands. The government made some rules concerning admission of Indo-Europeans that differed from the normal immigration policy applied to others, recognizing its moral obligation to the option-regretters if they were in a situation of need attributable to the Netherlands. Minister of Justice Samkalden, responsible for this policy, spoke of lack of juridical obligation but recognized "humanitarian grounds" and "needs and difficulties" of the Indo-Europeans.[2] The situation for the Indo-Europeans deteriorated in spite of their choice of Indonesian nationality, and by the end of 1957 the government was confronted with a stream of applications by option-regretters.

During 1957 Dutch firms in Indonesia were nationalized and the Dutch who remained there were declared persona non grata; 33,000 Dutch repatriated in the Netherlands. During 1959 the government formulated a new set of rules and allowed admission of an estimated 2,000 option-regretters per year. Then, in response to pressure from Parliament, the planned number was increased to 2,400. In 1960 the Van Vollenhoven committee was established to pass upon all applications which the department did not intend to admit at once. The end of the New Guinea conflict in 1962 was the direct cause of the termination of this policy. Applications by option-regretters were received

1. H. C. Wassenaar-Jellesma. Van Oost naar West, relaas van de repatriering van 1945 tot en met 1966. Uitgave Ministerie van Cultuur, Recreatie en Maatschappelijk Werk, Staatsdrukkerij, 1969.

2. Hand. IIe Kamer, zitting 1958–59, p. 2232. Hand. IIe Kamer, zitting 1960–61, MvA p. 1.

on a special basis until April, 1964, when the normal alien policy became applicable, except that within the general policy special rules for Indonesians were applied until the end of 1972.

Under this special program for option-regretters the government received more than 12,500 requests for admission. Approximately 6,000 applications were decided in favor of the applicants. Because most applications involved families, the result was the admission of more than 25,000 people to the Netherlands under this program.

THE LEGAL BACKGROUND

The 1892 Act on Dutch Nationality provides that one may obtain Dutch nationality by descent from Netherlands citizens, by living as aliens in the Netherlands for three generations, by naturalization, by adoption (since 1962), and by marriage (for women). The Act of 1892 did not apply to all inhabitants of the Dutch East Indies, but an Act of 1910 gave them the status of Dutch subjects. The three groups since 1910 are people with Dutch nationality, Dutch subjects without Dutch nationality, and aliens. The Indonesian independence treaty of 1949 provided that Indonesian inhabitants with Dutch nationality remained Dutch but in some cases could choose Indonesian nationality. Autochthonous Dutch subjects without Dutch nationality (those born of parents who were born in Indonesia) automatically became Indonesians. Foreign Dutch subjects who were born in Indonesia became Indonesians but could choose Dutch nationality if they had no other nationality. The option-regretters policy applied not only to those who chose Indonesian nationality and later regretted that they had not chosen Dutch nationality, but also to a group of "sociocultural" Dutch who had had no option but were closely related to the Dutch by education, religion, spiritual climate, work, or marriage.

The Aliens Act of 1849, supplemented in 1918 and 1939, required a visa for admission to the Netherlands, but it also in some circumstances allowed admission without a visa; admission of aliens for residence was allowed only for one year at a time, and denials were not subject to appeal. The main requirements for admission were sufficient means, no danger to the public order or security, and advantage to the Dutch society. The Minister thus had broad discretion. Within the boundaries of the law, he was completely free to grant or deny admission, except that since 1950 he has been required to seek advice from the Permanent Advice Committee on Aliens (P.V.A.C.) in a few cases.

NORMS OF ADMISSION

The Department of Justice recognized in 1956 that rules for option-regretters were necessary, and rules were issued on the basis of analysis of about a hundred dossiers. The rules were revised in 1959 and 1962. The 1962 rules provided that, in absence of serious doubt about adaptability to the Netherlands or other factors calling for non-admittance, applicants who are in needy circumstances and belong to the following categories can be considered for admission:

A. applicant born and educated in the Netherlands or has lived there more than ten years (including family of applicant);

B. parents of applicant born in the Netherlands with Dutch nationality (including family of applicant);

C. application of married couple of Dutch origin, both parents of one applicant originally being of Dutch nationality, and a child of the applicants is living in the Netherlands, or more of the parents of both applicants are living in the Netherlands than in Indonesia, or, if the parents are dead, there are no relatives of the second degree living in Indonesia but there are in the Netherlands (family of such applicant also admitted);

D. applicant a formerly married ex-Dutch national whose parents are both of Dutch nationality and applicant has no adult relatives living in Indonesia but has adult relatives of the first or second degree in the Netherlands (family also admitted);

E. applicant, an ex-Dutch national, never married, who has reached majority and whose parents are both of Dutch nationality and he has no relatives of the first or second degree living in Indonesia but has such relatives in the Netherlands;

F. applicant is a minor one of whose parents or foster parents is of Dutch nationality and applicant will live with such parent in the Netherlands, if departure of minor to the Netherlands will not break up the family (but whole family not considered for admittance);

G. applicant a part of family of Dutch origin and completely dependent on that family, even if that family left for the Netherlands after 1957, if applicant certainly will be living with and cared for by his family in the Netherlands;

H. applicants having Dutch passports and failing to opt in erroneous belief that passports meant they already had Dutch nationality (families of such applicants also admitted);

I. applicants opted for Dutch nationality, option at first considered valid by Dutch authorities but later ruled invalid (families also admitted);

J. applicants having very special merits for the Netherlands (families also admitted);

K. applicant fulfilled military duties and was prisoner of war and is or was married to wife of Dutch origin.

To be admitted, then, an applicant had to be (1) in one of the eleven categories from A to K, (2) adaptable to the Netherlands, (3) free from other factors calling for non-admittance, and (4) in needy circumstances. The last three requirements were given changing content in the course of time.

The applicant had the serious burden of proving that the facts fitted him into one of the eleven categories, and the governmental administration in Indonesia often had difficulty in supplying the needed data. The Minister of Justice resisted pressures to extend the categories; for instance, he refused to allow admission to one whose option was exercised for him because he was under age in 1950 and 1951. He defended his opinion by pointing out that the categories were used as guiding rules and were not strictly binding.

The vague concept of adaptability was gradually refined, but the refinements were never incorporated into the rules. Adaptability involved ties with the Netherlands and participation in Dutch (or Western) culture. Ties meant relatives in the Netherlands with whom the applicant had kept contact; the doubt-

ful cases were the ones in which about as many relatives were
in the Netherlands as in Indonesia. The cultural factors included being educated in a Dutch way, as in a Protestant or
Catholic mission in Indonesia; milieu; a Christian conviction;
being orphans reared in Dutch institutions, or members of
other special groups; having political opinions indicating affilia-
tion with Western culture; and the absence of a negative
reason, such as a completely non-Western view of marriage and
sexual relations.

Factors calling for non-admittance included an anti-Dutch
attitude (such as collaborating with the Japanese during
World War II, or the role played during the struggle for Indonesian independence); conviction for crime; connection with
prostitution or other undesirable activity; attitudes about other
applicants (including blackmail or exposure of others to social
risk by disclosing their applications).

The Dutch government acknowledged its moral obligation
to the option-regretters. "Needy circumstances" included social
pressures from neighbors or colleagues in Indonesia, illness
coupled with inadequacy of medical service, threats of violence,
dependency on relatives in the Netherlands, employers' discrimination against Indo-Europeans, employment well below
the individual's capacity, unbearable living conditions, and
living on pensions which become grossly inadequate through
Indonesian inflation. At first only the most poignant cases were
considered for admission, but the lesser forms of deprivation
later became enough to satisfy the requirement for admission.

A 1959 rule said that an applicant could be admitted if he
had "ample means" for travel, food, and lodging. Normally
the Dutch government paid the travel expenses to the Netherlands for those unable to pay. The files give the impression that
decisions were more favorable for those who were able to pay
their own expenses, yet the Minister of Justice explicitly said
exactly the opposite to Parliament in 1961.

The use of quotas probably delayed admissions, even though
only a few applicants were excluded through use of quotas.
Successive ministers have acknowledged the use of quotas. Samkalden: "37,000 Dutch will be received . . . the question is

how far the promised increase of the quota can be realized." [3] Struycken: ". . . a maximum number of admissions from Indonesia of approximately 150 persons per month . . . it is decided to double the number of admissions for this year." [4] Beerman: "In 1958 the number was 1,200; in 1959 the number will be 2,000." [5] An explanation that these numbers are only estimates, without any further significance, seems improbable. This explanation would be valid only if the development of the rules had been such that the mentioned numbers would be the result of them. One is probably close to the truth in saying that the numbers were estimates which were not intended to be deviated from too much.

Along with the four general norms for admission, there were the two special norms—the applicant's financial status and the quota. But even the categories were less than absolute; belonging to a category was not always essential for admission. When the Van Vollenhoven committee was established, the Minister said explicitly that the rules were guiding principles. An applicant who did not fit a category could be admitted if the case is of the type covered by the categories. The 1959 rules contained an explicit provision allowing admission of an applicant not fitting a category, on the basis of special and difficult circumstances, if a link existed between the rules and the applicant's condition. That provision was omitted from the 1962 rules, probably because it was superfluous for rules that were deemed guiding principles.

The Minister's and administrators' discretion was less before 1959 than later. The rules governed at first; later they were used only as guides for discretion. For instance, the ten-year requirement of category A could sometimes be satisfied by eight or nine years. Positive factors could be weighed against negative ones; the case of a prostitute who speaks Dutch and has relatives in the Netherlands involves a weighing of the positive against the negative, as does the case of one who opposed the Japanese in World War II, later worked for the nationalists

3. Hand. IIe Kamer, zitting 1958–59, p. 2232.
4. *Id.*, p. 2180.
5. *Id.*, p. 2144.

against the Netherlands, and finally in the conflict between Indonesia and the Netherlands about New Guinea considered the Indonesian position unreasonable. Such terms as "need" and "adaptability" necessarily required exercise of discretion.

Here is an example showing the range for discretion. An applicant has lived in the Netherlands for seven years. He has a Dutch education and he speaks Dutch. But his only relatives live in Indonesia. No negative factors are known about him. He lives in relative affluence in Indonesia. He comes close to category A. Adaptability seems assured, but the ties with the Netherlands are lacking. Need is doubtful. The administrator could put more weight on ties and less on Western culture and could emphasize that need was doubtful, or he could put the accent on Western culture and adaptability and he could assume need and emphasize that the ten-year requirement of category A was approximately met.

ORGANIZATION, PROCEDURE, AND OPENNESS

In the Department of Justice is a special division of alien affairs and frontier custody. The section of alien affairs has several bureaus, one of which is a bureau for Indonesian cases. The Minister was advised by the Permanente Vreemfelingen Advies Commissie (P.V.A.C.); a subcommittee, known as the Van Vollenhoven committee, advised on option-regretters. To investigate facts about applications, the department used police and social advisers, as well as contacts in Indonesia. Before 1960 and after 1963 the diplomatic personnel in Djakarta played a minor role in this policy; their main function was as go-between.[6]

Applications were made to the Dutch embassy in Djakarta. The embassy then sent them to the Hague, where the Department of Justice classified them and instituted investigations which were carried out mostly by police, social advisers, and contacts in Indonesia. The lower administrators made a recommendation to admit or deny admission, and the decision was

6. Between 1960 and 1963 diplomatic relations between Indonesia and the Netherlands were cut off.

then usually made by either the head of the Indonesian bureau or the head of the section of alien affairs. Difficult cases often went to higher administrators, and in a few instances to the Minister. The Minister would usually decide the cases that were likely to create new precedents. The Van Vollenhoven committee began in 1961 to pass upon cases that were tentative denials.

Remarkably little information about the reasons for decisions is in the dossiers. Short notes of lower administrators with a short remark of the deciding administrator are usual. During the early period the Van Vollenhoven committee gave ample reasons for its advice, but later the reasons became shorter and often were meaningless standard formulas. Even when the committee's advice was rejected, the deciding officer often would not give detailed written reasons. Even when reasons were stated, they were never given to applicants.

Interventions were often made on behalf of applicants by members of Parliament, by representatives of pressure groups, and by relatives or friends of applicants. One or two members of Parliament had regular meetings with administrators and occasional meetings with the Minister, making arguments for admission of particular applicants. Pressures from members of Parliament were entirely on the side of admitting applicants, not on the side of denying applications. The two pressure groups, C.C.K.P. and NASSI, became proficient in helping applicants and in 1961 got confidential copies of the rules; the organizations were also able to compare one application with another, and with prior decisions about which they had information. We have not been able to establish that the various interventions caused substantial changes in or departures from the admission policy.

Administrators took into account known precedents; they were usually bound by them but could nevertheless bring about changes in policy through individual decisions. The policy about option-regretters was constantly changing. All the major changes were toward a more lenient policy. Such changes did not mean that precedents favorable to applicants became ineffective; changes could sometimes be brought about by following one set of precedents instead of another.

Appeals from denials were not allowed until 1964,[7] when the General Appeal Act allowed appeals to the Crown (the Queen and the responsible Minister), on advice of a section of the Council of State. The only ground for reversal was illegality. Yet about 20 percent of appeals by option-regretters have been successful, as compared with only 6 percent of other cases under the General Appeal Act. Some holdings of illegality are based on violations of the principle of equality. Appeals, however, had little effect on policy, because they began in 1964, the year in which the special program for option-regretters ended.

Even the rules stating the categories for admission were kept secret. When in 1959–60 M.P. Van Doorn pleaded in Parliament for publication of the rules on the grounds of "considerations of fairness" and need for closer parliamentary control of the policy,[8] Minister of Justice Beerman answered that publication of the rules "might give rise to unjustified expectations and a new unrest" and that "there are existing here absolutely no tendencies to autocratic administration."[9]

Planning during 1963 to end the option-regretters policy was secret. Then, about January 1, 1964, an announcement was widely publicized in Indonesia that applications had to be made before April 1, 1964.

EVALUATION

The option-regretters policy was less planned than it could have been, and less planned than it at first appeared to be. The policy was unstable as a result of inadequate planning and lack of a clear interrelation between the quota and the rules.

The categories confined discretion in the early stages when they governed the results, but later they confined discretion less. Our opinion is that the administration should have extended the categories instead of departing from them. For instance, instead of interpreting the ten-year requirement of category A to mean eight or nine years, it might have been amended

7. Before 1964, in case of a denial a renewed request was the only possible way to get a decision reversed.
8. Hand. IIe Kamer, zitting 1959–60, p. 2145.
9. *Id.*

to require five or six years, and then it might have been applied according to its terms.

Similarly, the term "adaptability" has been given meaning by creating various criteria. We believe it regrettable that the criteria were not included in the rules. The same is true of the concepts of "need" and "other factors."

Amending the rules is preferable to adding to their meaning through practice, because absence of reasons for decisions means that the precedents are not readily accessible to administrators and that the precedents accordingly have little value as guides. We do not mean that all discretion should be eliminated through perfecting the rules; we mean only that unnecessary discretion should be eliminated.

The probable reason for the administrators' failure to change the rules is that they preferred to maintain their discretionary power. Discretion allowed them to carry out the policy they liked. Their attitude was consistent with their good faith, because they were convinced that in that way the policy would best be implemented.

The financial position of the applicant may also have had some influence on the decisions. If it did, the decisions were not in accord with the basis of this policy. Some administrators argued that more detailed rules would have to be applied more strictly, but we think that argument unsound because any rules, whether detailed or general, can be applied either strictly or leniently. Quotas may have had some effect on discretionary choices, and the quotas may have caused postponement of admission of some applicants, but we think it unlikely that quotas caused many permanent denials.

Making the needed investigations in Indonesia was often difficult, and the results were not always satisfactory. The investigation of relatives in the Netherlands was unsatisfactory because it was based on grounds irrelevant to the decisions. The dossiers of individual applicants contained all the material available for decision, but the facts generally were not arranged systematically in the files, even though such arrangement was essential for orderly decision-making and for review of decisions.

The administrators defended their practice of giving no reasons for decisions by saying that they had no time to state reasons in all cases, and that giving reasons was unnecessary. Failure to state reasons is one of the most serious flaws in the system. Applicants were unnecessarily frustrated and damaged —they were entitled to make new applications, but they had no way of knowing which points to emphasize, and they could not determine whether a decision had been made on a false or insufficient ground. Internally the omission of reasons hampered the influence of precedents and hierarchical checking.

Decisions were never made public. Perhaps names of those denied admission should not be publicized, for some applicants do not want their desire to leave Indonesia to be known. Yet reasoned opinions could be made public, for use as precedents, with names deleted. The interest in having useful precedents is thus not necessarily incompatible with full protection of the interest in privacy.

Decisions were used internally as precedents, but they were mostly inaccessible because they were not systematically stored. A remedy could be to designate some decisions as precedents, and then to keep that collection of decisions indexed and available to all officers who participate in decision-making. As the decisions moved away from the original meaning of the rules, the rules became more and more misleading. It seems incomprehensible that the administrators themselves did not realize that they were following a bad system; our guess is that they supposed they could sufficiently remember the precedents, but we strongly doubt that this was possible.

Decisions of lower officials have been reviewed by their superiors in a hierarchical organization headed by the Minister; after 1964, even the Minister's decision was subject to appeal. The checks at various levels were undoubtedly a safeguard against arbitrariness or inequality—yet superiors were dependent on the information which their subordinates provided, and precedents were often inaccessible, so the checking was less than fully effective.

Few policy statements were openly made before 1963. Speeches in Parliament often advocated a more liberal admission policy, although no overall plan for treatment of option-regretters was ever published. The Minister evidently believed that his policies were more likely to prevail if they were largely secret. Publication of a plan would have furthered parliamentary guidance for policy-making and would have helped the option-regretters to evaluate their prospects. Some administrators told us that no plans existed, but that seems to be contradicted by the rules and quotas. We must conclude that the government failed with regard to supplying information about its plans and intentions. Parliament also failed, for though it made some objections to the secrecy, it never made the lack of openness a fundamental issue.

The fact that the rules were not published seems especially unfortunate. Arguments were made in Parliament that the government made it impossible for the option-regretters to appraise their chances, to prove their eligibility, or even to establish a basis for criticizing the policy. The argument that knowledge of the rules would have encouraged falsifying of facts seems without merit. It is doubtful that there ever was cheating on a large scale. The argument that the option-regretters would have misunderstood the rules seems beneath contempt; the argument that publication of rules would have increased the number of applications may be valid, but, if so, the secrecy meant discouragement of applications that were possibly justified. The moral obligation to the option-regretters could be satisfied only by full disclosure of the policy to those affected by it; publication of the rules also would have meant a better parliamentary and public understanding of what the government was doing. Secrecy meant that the debates were often frustrating for both the Parliament and the Minister. Although the Minister in 1961 supplied the rules in confidence to the Repatriation Committee of the Second Chamber and to the C.C.K.P. and NASSI pressure groups, the acceptance of confidentiality had the unfortunate effect of cutting off criticism of the rules and made general criticism of the policy difficult.

SUMMARY

We unhesitatingly find that unnecessary discretionary power in administering the option-regretters policy resulted in unjust decisions. The discretion was too broad, and the administrators did not do enough to confine it. The policy development began with recognition of the moral obligation of the Netherlands to the option-regretters. The written rules initially served as a good instrument to confine discretion, but the next step should have been to clarify "adaptability," "need," and "other factors," and that was never done. Use of vague standards was justified at the outset, but not after enough cases had been decided to furnish the basis for clarification. In the later phases of the program, the clarification that the rules had accomplished was not increased, as it should have been through reliance on the accumulating experience; rather, it was diminished by the discretionary departures from the plain meaning of the rules.

Discretion should have been confined by further refinement of the rules, and by reasoned opinions which could have served as precedents. The lack of either type of confinement was aggravated by the secrecy of both the rules and the precedents. Planning, including estimates and quotas, should have been openly done all along the line. Instead, openness ended with little more than the early recognition of the moral obligation, the public statements about quotas, and the final statement ending the policy.

Findings and reasons should have been systematically stated in individual cases. Findings usually were not systematically stated, and the factual contents of files were usually not systematically arranged. Reasons either were not stated at all or were so summary that one could not glean from them an understanding of the decision. The findings and reasons should have been open to public inspection, with names deleted to protect privacy. A system of open precedents would have reduced unguided discretion, while still allowing discretionary power to change a policy for reasons adequately explained. The checking of decisions of lower administrators was reduced in effectiveness by the lack of systematic findings or reasons, and even by the lack of a systematic arrangement of files. The check provided through allowing appeals to the Crown, which began in 1964, was desirable and might well have come earlier, for the experience with the appeals—a 20 percent reversal rate—proved that such additional checking was needed.

American Comments on Dutch Option-Regretters

Mr. Scheffers and his associates state a strong conclusion: "We unhesitatingly find that unnecessary discretionary power in administering the option-regretters policy resulted in unjust decisions."

That conclusion, in my opinion, says a very great deal. It says that unjust decisions result from unnecessary power. It says that ordinary administrators within the Dutch Ministry of Justice are likely to provide a better quality of justice if their unnecessary discretionary power is cut back. It says that such administrators, with no special spur from the outside, do not voluntarily confine their own discretion to eliminate what is unnecessary; instead, they exercise the discretion in ways that independent scholars find to be unjust. From my point of view, then, Dutch administrators are about the same as American administrators. The sameness may lie in the fact that both are human beings. And the ultimate truth may be that human nature is incompatible with unnecessary discretionary power.

More broadly, the basic truth may be that unnecessary discretionary power should be eliminated, and that necessary discretionary power should be confined, structured, and checked.

The Dutch Ministry of Justice did confine the discretion with written rules. That helped. But the rules were gradually violated, and the discretion again became broader.

Discretion could have been confined and structured by reasoned opinions and by a system of precedents. But busy administrators, either in the Netherlands or in the United States, do not of their own volition confine or structure their unnecessary discretionary power. They do not do open planning. They do not open their policies to public inspection and public criticism. Someone with a different perspective is needed to prod the administrators to confine and to structure their discretion. The Minister did not do that. The Members of Parliament did not. And the right to appeal to the Crown did not accomplish that, for the right of appeal did not come until the last year of the program. If it had come sooner, the confining and structuring might have been required in time to prevent a good deal of injustice.

Those are the lessons to be learned, in my opinion, from the well-told story of the option-regretters. But I think one more lesson can be gleaned from that story: if the ultimate purpose of Europeans and Americans who are engaged in legal education is to understand the problems of how to administer justice and to minimize injustice, and to convey that understanding to students and to others, as I think it is, then it seems to me that the essay on the option-regretters raises the question whether legal education, both in Europe and in America, must include problems of justice and injustice in administration, not merely problems of justice and injustice in the review of administration.

CHAPTER TEN

Overall Perspective

KENNETH CULP DAVIS

Two major conclusions emerge from this study, neither of which was foreseen at the outset. Because of good luck, and not good planning, one major conclusion happens to involve what Americans can learn from Europeans, and the other happens to involve what Europeans can learn from Americans.

Before I state the conclusions, I should explain that many conclusions of narrower scope have value but are not now summarized because most of them are better understood in their contexts. And I should also like to acknowledge that the hypothesis with which we started was abandoned at an early time. If Europeans have special insights about discretion that Americans lack, it has not come to light in our eight samples of European discretionary justice. The samples are too limited to support a finding that the hypothesis is disproved; experience we have not examined could support it.

THE AMERICAN SYSTEM OF PROSECUTING

The first major conclusion is that American attitudes and practices concerning uncontrolled discretion of prosecutors should be reexamined in the light of the system of the German prosecutor. That conclusion is far more than a confirmation of the belief which I already had when planning this study; what is added is not only new, but also unanticipated. I now believe, on the basis of the more thorough and more detailed inquiry, that the American system of prosecuting is not merely inferior but grossly inferior, and that the need for comprehensive re-examination is not merely reasonably clear but overwhelming.

This symposium includes three treatments of European prosecuting power—Professor Herrmann's on the German prosecutor, Mr. Meessen's on administration of antitrust law in the European Communities, and Mr. Staatsen's on enforcement of the Nuisance Act in the Netherlands. The three together show that European attitudes about prosecuting are variable and may sometimes resemble American attitudes. The system that contrasts the most with the American system is that of the German prosecutor. The reasons for the major conclusion I have stated are spelled out above in my commentary on Professor Herrmann's essay. I shall not try to summarize them here, except to point out that the section entitled "The Dozen Facets of Uncontrolled Discretion" of the American prosecutor not only contrasts in general with the next section entitled "The German Controlled Discretion," but it contrasts with respect to *every one of the dozen items.*

The section entitled "Some Questions about Future Planning" identifies over two dozen specific questions for American consideration. I do not try to answer those questions; they must be answered through many groups, many studies, many debates. The first step has to be to open up the problems for consideration. Even that much involves difficulty, because as of today almost every member of the American legal profession "knows" that prosecutor's discretion must be nearly unlimited and almost completely unguided. I am now convinced that that view is based on unplanned drift over many generations. We Americans must replace our long-term false assumptions with a full understanding of realities and potentialities. That we will copy the German system seems quite unlikely; that we will draw guidance and inspiration from it seems to me clearly desirable.

The neglected discretionary power on which we should especially focus is *discretion not to enforce*—which, strangely, is not merely the other side of the discretion-to-enforce coin. The negative power is much less controlled than the affirmative power, in that it is usually final instead of interim, it is usually secret instead of intrinsically open, it is much less likely to be governed or guided by standards or principles, and it is much less often supported by findings or reasons.

What I am calling "prosecuting" should be interpreted broadly to include all law enforcement by public authority. It involves many more officers than those we call prosecutors. Prosecuting agencies include police agencies, licensing agencies, regulatory agencies, agencies which award subsidies or grants, and even welfare agencies. The American need to re-examine discretion to prosecute or not to prosecute extends to all prosecuting in that broad sense.

Unreviewed Discretionary Action in Europe

The second major conclusion is that Europeans should inquire into the question whether they should give more attention to problems of justice in administration, as distinguished from problems of justice in administrative courts. European administrative law consists almost entirely of what administrative courts do. Should it be expanded to include what administrative courts *do not do* to correct injustice in administration?

That question can be broken down into four subordinate questions: (1) How extensive are problems of administrative justice that never or almost never come before administrative courts? (2) Should administrative courts create more procedural law that is generally applicable to administrators and not limited to particular cases? (3) Should Europeans make studies of the 98 or 99 percent of administrative action, whether or not discretionary, that is not *in fact* reviewed by administrative courts? (4) Do university faculties and students have a role to play in investigating and studying problems of justice in administration that do not come before administrative courts? I shall now consider each of these four questions.

(1) The quality of justice in administrative courts is high. But what is the quality of justice in administration, and what portion of problems of justice in administration are never considered by administrative courts? This question does not seem to be answered in the literature of European administrative law. Does the total system largely fail in the cases that are not brought to administrative courts?

The kinds of administrative action that never or almost never reach administrative courts are quite extensive and vital.

Ready examples are the multi-billion-lire program of subsidies for the development of southern Italy, and the multi-billion-franc program of tax relief contracts in France. The Italian program began in 1950; the French program, in 1938. The effects of both programs on many corporations have been of great magnitude. But both programs are almost untouched by the work of the Consiglio di Stato or of the Conseil d'Etat. In the Italian program, as Professor Cassese's essay shows, rules do not govern the amounts of grants; reasons are not stated to disappointed applicants; discretion is not guided by standards or rules or precedents; and administrators maintain almost complete secrecy about recipients and amounts. Yet the Consiglio di Stato, partly for lack of opportunity, has done nothing to correct such administrative deficiencies. Mr. Merlin's paper on the French program brings out that the Ministry of Finance, with no disapproval by the Conseil d'Etat, keeps secret such rules and guides as it uses in awarding tax relief contracts, typically gives no reasons for its decisions, is unguided by its own precedents, and has no special incentive to avoid doing more for one corporation than for another in similar circumstances. Yet review by the Conseil d'Etat has been almost zero, despite the broad and unguided discretion and despite the huge amounts involved. In 1963 a French association applied pressure on the Ministry of Finance to adopt a system of stating reasons, but the Ministry refused. The issue was a vital one. But the Conseil d'Etat *in fact* played no role in it.

Nearly all administration is *in theory* subject to review by administrative courts. In France, for instance, all administrative acts are reviewable except "actes de gouvernement" and "mesures d'ordre intérieur administratives"—acts of government and an agency's internal management measures. Both categories are quite narrow. Other administrative courts similarly have few and narrow limitations on their jurisdiction to review all administrative action. What seems to me especially important is the common European assumption that what is reviewable determines what is reviewed. But I am inclined to raise the question whether a very large portion of European administrative action that is reviewable—perhaps as much as half

—is never or almost never reviewed. For instance, consider the half-dozen illustrations of discretionary injustice set out in the first section of the first chapter—the policeman's arrest of one boy and not the other, the agency's investigation of one polluter and not the other, the welfare claimant who does not know how to appeal, different treatment of two embezzlers, the unlawful grant of a subsidy to a competitor, and admission of one alien and the exclusion of another. In all such illustrations, administrative courts *in fact* play no role (with an exception in Germany concerning the subsidy).

How many programs, like the two very large ones in Italy and France, are *in fact* never or almost never subject to review? Mr. Scheffers's conclusion in his study of the Dutch program of the option-regretters is: "We unhesitatingly find that unnecessary discretionary power in administering the option-regretters policy resulted in unjust decisions." But the unjust decisions were not corrected by a reviewing authority. Was the theory at variance with the reality? Out of 11,654 general assistance cases in one year in the Netherlands, only one case was appealed to the Crown; yet Mr. Staatsen finds that some officers are "hawks" who regard public assistance as a privilege, and some are "doves" who deem benefits too low and seize every opportunity to try to increase them, but that such differences are not always ironed out, so that the result in a particular case may depend upon which officer happens to handle it. Even when administrators do such a splendid job that review is hardly ever needed, as in the case of the Danish Family Guidance Center in Copenhagen, the theory that justice comes from reviewing courts is at variance with the reality. Mr. Busck says that no case has gone from that Center either to the courts or to the ombudsman. Do not administrators' successes, as well as their failures, call for study?

(2) One main difference between French or German administrative law and American administrative law is the extent to which administrative or other courts create principles that control administration in cases resembling the ones decided by the courts. American courts create a great deal of procedural law which is fully applicable to all administrative action that

comes within the principles enunciated by the courts. But French or German administrative courts create such procedural law only to a relatively small extent. The control of administration through principles of law is thus relatively large in America and relatively limited in France and Germany. I must repeat that nearly two-thirds of my multi-volume *Administrative Law Treatise* is devoted to the law of administrative procedure that has been developed by reviewing courts in America—law that controls any and all administrators whenever it is applicable. But the French and German treatises on administrative law contain hardly any counterpart of such case law. The European conception of "administrative procedure" does not generally include procedure that administrators are required to use; it relates primarily to procedure of administrative courts. The lack of a large body of case law in Europe to govern the procedure of administrators has always seemed strange to my American eyes. When a party before an American reviewing court asserts procedural unfairness in the administrative process, the court normally decides the procedural question, thereby creating a precedent to guide all administrators who are confronted by that question. How often does a European administrative court in the same circumstances ignore the procedural question and finally dispose of the case on the merits, substituting its own procedure for the assertedly faulty procedure of the administrator, and thus never making a decision on the procedural question? Administrative courts, especially recently, do sometimes decide procedural questions, thereby creating procedural law. In France, for instance, the Conseil d'Etat has boldly developed a few *principes generaux du droit;* in Germany, the general principles may be slightly more extensive. I think that is precisely what is needed. But should what I regard as a relatively tiny amount of such procedural case law be vastly expanded? I think it should be, and predict that it will be.

Perhaps the French and the Germans are in the early stages of exploiting the simple proposition that doing justice in the first instance—in the administration—is about a hundred times as important quantitatively as correction of administrative injustice by a reviewing authority. Once that simple proposition is fully accepted, as I think it is destined to be, no significant barriers will stand in the way of the development of a full set of principles that surely will be superior to what administrators generally do when they act without the guidance of such principles. That the administrative courts are already creating general principles, either in the name of statutory interpretation or simply as a matter of doing justice in the cases they decide, shows that no constitutional limitation prevents such creativity. Indeed, the recent holding of the French Constitutional Council that the principle of equality even limits Parliament may add to the tools of the Conseil d'Etat, because the principle of equality, like American due process, is potentially a basis for further *principes generaux*.

(3) Probably in both Europe and America, not more than 1 or 2 percent of administrative action reaches administrative or other courts. In legal literature and in legal education both Europeans and Americans give a great deal of attention to that 1 or 2 percent. As for the 98 or 99 percent, Americans investigate and study it, but Europeans generally do not. A part of the question I am raising is whether Europeans should give much more attention to administrative action that does not reach administrative or other courts.

Americans, in and out of government, often interview administrators and prepare descriptive and critical studies. The Attorney General's Committee on Administrative Procedure prepared about fifty monographs, each on one agency and each based on extensive interviews with administrators, as a basis for its influential 1941 report. The first and second Hoover Commissions in the late 1940s and early 1950s made similar though less comprehensive studies. The temporary Administrative Conferences of the federal government made such studies in the 1960s, and now the permanent Administrative Conference of the United States, made up of about eighty people, the majority of whom are in government service, has been making or sponsoring many such studies since 1968. Our bar associations often investigate administration and recommend changes in practices or changes in legislation about administrative practices. Public discussion not only of administrative policies but also of administrative practices is very common.

Are similar investigations of administration needed in Europe? They are not totally absent now, but almost. Administrative procedure legislation has been considered here and there, with some slight adoptions. The ombudsman idea is spreading; the British Parliamentary Commissioner and the new French Médiateur may prove to be quite important. But the basic fact remains that I have been unable to find any European empirical study of discretionary justice. How much correctible injustice might such studies bring to light? No one knows. My American experience and our eight samples of European administration lead me to estimate that it might be considerable. What reforms might follow? Might a good deal of unnecessary discretionary power be cut back? Would many areas of secret administrative action be opened to public inspection and public criticism? Would more standards and more rules be formulated to guide discretionary action? Would administrators more often be required to state findings and reasons to disappointed parties? Would administrators be required to follow their own precedents or to explain why they are departing from them? What other ways of protecting against discretionary injustice might European inventiveness create?

(4) My opinion is that faculties and students in educational institutions of all countries should study detailed governmental processes, as well as the detailed substantive materials of those processes. The faculties, as well as the students, should be informed critics of the administrators and of the administrative processes. Informed criticism can improve both the quality of justice in administration and its effectiveness. Universities and government administrators have much to offer to each other.

Perhaps for some Europeans the most important single fact brought out by the present study is a very simple one that could quickly have been found without our long investigation: *People in universities can learn about governmental processes by talking with people in government offices.* In our eight studies, no administrator has placed obstacles in the way of our interviewing. That European administrators are amenable to being interviewed seems to me to be a fact of great consequence. No longer do European studies of discretion and its control need to be wholly abstract. They can be based on the realities of administration.

If European scholars will on a broad scale make studies by interviewing administrators, might not both the governmental benefits and the educational benefits be enormous?